P9-ELT-782

MAKING PLAYS

The editor Colin Chambers is the Literary Manager of the Royal Shakespeare Company. Since joining the company in 1980 he has been involved in the production of more than 75 new plays, including six by Richard Nelson. He has written about contemporary theatre for newspapers, magazines and journals, and is the author of the following: *Theatre London* (editor, 1980); *Other Spaces: New Theatre and the RSC* (1980); *Dreams and Deconstructions* (contributor, 1980); *Playwrights' Progress: Patterns of Postwar British Drama* (co-author, 1987); *The Story of Unity Theatre* (1989); *Heart of a Heartless World: Essays in Cultural Resistance* (contributor, 1995).

MAKING PLAYS

The Writer–Director Relationship in the Theatre Today

Richard Nelson & David Jones

EDITED BY COLIN CHAMBERS

faber and faber
LONDON · BOSTON

First published in 1995
by Faber and Faber Limited
3 Queen Square London WC1N 3AU

Phototypeset by Datix International, Bungay, Suffolk
Printed in England by Clays Ltd, St Ives plc

All rights reserved

© David Jones, Richard Nelson and Colin Chambers 1995
Foreword © Trevor Nunn 1995
Extract from *The Honourable Beast*, published by Nick Hern Books Ltd,
London, © 1993 Riggs O'Hara and the estate of John Dexter; extract from
Timebends by Arthur Miller by kind permission of Methuen

Richard Nelson and David Jones are hereby identified as
authors of this work in accordance with Section 77 of the
Copyright, Designs and Patents Act 1988.

A CIP record for this book is available
from the British Library

ISBN 0 571 16354 8

10 9 8 7 6 5 4 3 2 1

For Those Who Come After

Joe, Jesse
Beth, Ben
Zoe, Jocelyn

Contents

Foreword by Trevor Nunn   ix

Acknowledgements   xii

Introduction *by Richard Nelson*   xiii

ONE   Keats's Theory of Negative Capability:
David Jones on Playwrights   1

TWO   Close to Death: Richard Nelson on Directors   26

THREE   Stupid Questions: the Text   48

FOUR   Two Amazing White Breasts and a Large Piece
of Coal: Designing the Play   78

FIVE   Eating Out Together: Casting and Rehearsals   88

SIX   A Lot of Fear in the Air: Producers, Previews
and Critics   109

SEVEN   Feeling Hurt and Betrayed?: the Future
Relationship   129

EIGHT   An Old Marriage: *Misha's Party*   142

Biographical Note: David Jones   157

Biographical Note: Richard Nelson   162

Foreword

Theatre is writing on the sand, vulnerable to the next incoming tide, and in the case of books about the theatre probably to the next wave, so quickly do ideas change. This is not a complaint. Theatre is a highly collaborative activity in which writers, directors, designers and actors pool their skills and insights in the full knowledge that compromise is often present in the result. Those collaborations would all become intolerably more difficult if they were to be saddled with the notion that the result was for posterity.

Theatre is for now. Classic plays change their meaning from decade to decade and the best revivals are the ones that respond to the new prism through which the old work is viewed. Most new plays don't survive the test of time, as political and philosophical fashions are supplanted in the perpetual ebb and flow of intellectual manners and mores. Witness, most recently, the vast volume of Marxist-inspired revolutionary and radical drama of the '60s and '70s which is now virtually unperformable after the discrediting of Eastern Bloc communist and socialist regimes that attended the collapse of the Soviet Union.

There is one particular book I keep always close to hand as a *memento mori* or at least a cautionary influence. It is an affectionately written English theatrical memoir of the 1920s and '30s, brightly confident that the names that spill out of every page are going to be familiar for generations to come. And the fact is, there is not a single name from cover to cover that, sixty years later, anyone has ever heard of. It could be a translation of the Albanian theatre year book.

But this book by two of my dearest friends, David Jones and Richard Nelson, seems to me to acknowledge these truths as self-evident throughout. Constructing their book with conversations, discussions, arguments and anecdotes that allow us to eavesdrop on the transitory play-making business, the writers insist on not taking themselves too seriously. It will be instructive and provocative to those involved in making and remaking plays, and revealing to those audience devotees out there in the dark who yearn to know more of what lies behind what they are watching. And for anybody who reads it, it should be a good laugh.

But beware, gentle reader, of believing that what these two gentlemen tell you is the truth. Any instruction by anecdote relies on that most fallible of human faculties, the memory. A massive folklore exists in the theatre which is unrecognizably debased by false attributions and exaggerations for the sake of a good yarn. At a more mundane level, I have found when reminiscing with theatre colleagues we produce contradictory accounts and bizarre reworkings of events as others recall them. The penchant for hyperbole (theirs or mine) becomes far more important than the dull grey facts. Theatre history is by definition impressionistic, unreliable and something between careless and carefree.

For example, my simple endeavour to distract an under-standably frightened friend as he contemplated plunging to the bottom of a two-hundred-foot lift shaft is rendered in these pages as evidence of the obsessive selfishness which characterizes all directors ... Well, between you and me, Richard Nelson wouldn't be a writer at all if he didn't fantasize and exaggerate.

David Jones I know like a second self; for a number of years, and with astonishingly relaxed expertise, he controlled the London end of the Royal Shakespeare Company and was my mentor, guide, travelling companion and much-loved colleague. He left to run a company of his own in Brooklyn, where one of the first people he appointed was Richard Nelson to be his dramaturg. In the smaller-than-normal world of the theatre, it wasn't long before I too sought to collaborate with Richard both on stage and screen, and ever since I have cherished his friendship and consulted his wisdom on life, both professional and personal. From hundreds of hours of experience, then, I know David and Richard to be superb conversationalists, which means that as well as being effortlessly articulate they are interested and patient listeners.

The best thing about the great works of theatrical theory, such as Stanislavski's *My Life in Art* or Brecht's *The Messingkauf Dialogues* or Brook's *The Empty Space*, is that they give us that unfakable sense of being there, partaking in the process and experiencing the judgements; but there is also a worst thing about these books, which is the 'disciples' they create, the imitators who elevate the book to the status of a Bible, and insist that from now on theirs is the only way. So please read this book critically, contentiously and undogmatically, and by so doing you will please the authors no end.

Their book is of now – spontaneous and vigorous and healthily opinionated. And at present, the tide is all the way out.

Trevor Nunn

Acknowledgements

We would like to thank the following: Victoria Buxton, Judy Daish, Ben Jancovich, Patricia Macnaughton, Cynthia Nelson, Frank Pike, Tracey Scoffield, Jane Tassell and Linda Theisen.

Introduction *by Richard Nelson*

As I remember it, David Jones and I had the idea for this book while having a drink at the Beekman Arms Tavern, a historic inn near my home in upstate New York which David calls 'America's Oldest Bar'. Typically, we were talking about work; I about an impending production of a play of mine to be directed by someone other than David; David about a project he was working on with another writer. As we spoke, an interesting truth about our work lives revealed itself – as a playwright I have watched a great many directors work but never another playwright, and David, as a director, has worked with many different playwrights but has only rarely seen a colleague in action.

I suppose that this realization should not have come as a surprise. Rehearsals of plays usually take place in an atmosphere where an outsider is seen as a distraction, and another director or playwright wishing to observe could qualify as a complete disruption. So I would guess that most playwrights and directors have gained most of their experience of making plays from productions that they either wrote or directed themselves. Making plays, like making love, requires both instinct and a willingness to learn from our partners. And perhaps the reason why we rarely speak about the collaborative process of producing a play is that we are intimidated by our ignorance of how others have done it!

Once I realized that David knew so much about 'how other writers do it', I wanted to ask a hundred questions. How do other writers behave in rehearsals? How do they handle rewrites? Cuts? Disagreements about meaning? Were they ever involved in design? In casting? How did they get on with producers? Did they give notes to actors? If not, how did they get out of it? And so on. My questions were always about the nuts and bolts of working in the theatre as a playwright rather than the metaphysics of drama. Writers are guarded and jealous people, eager to present themselves as above the fray; in David, I had found someone who could tell me their secrets – or at least give me insights into how other writers handled the problems and anxieties of having their plays brought to life by other people.

David, too, had his curiosity aroused, in his case about other directors and, specifically, about how *they* handled writers. We began to ask each other questions, to tell each other anecdotes; and soon we began to wonder if the stories we were telling were part of a larger tale.

The writer–director relationship is a defining feature of twentieth-century theatre, and the association of a writer with a particular director is a purely modern phenomenon. No textbook on modern drama can be complete without addressing this relationship, yet the simple question of how such a collaboration functions has rarely been discussed – such concerns as: what is a writer's role in rehearsal? where do the boundaries of the writer–director relationship lie and when are they over-stepped? how much of a director's personal experience is brought to bear in defining the meaning of a play?

As in any relationship, personality is a major factor and every collaboration uniquely reflects the personalities of the writer and director involved. As we continued our discussion, however, David and I began to wonder if our personal experiences revealed not only our own histories but also a process undergone by other writers and directors as well; a process which has played a significant part in making the theatre what it is today.

We decided to trace the relationships we have had with other writers and directors as well as with each other over the last fifteen years, hoping that a picture would emerge which, if not always pretty, would at least be true. We agreed to begin by discussing 'first meetings' – when a play is first read by the director, and when the writer first meets the director and learns what he thinks (or what the director says he thinks, or what the director wants the writer to think he thinks). From there we follow the process through revisions, rehearsals, previews and notices to the question of whether the relationship is one worth continuing. In an epilogue we follow the same story from the beginning again, tracing the relationship through one specific production, directed by David and written (with Alexander Gelman) by me.

Our first session was held in October 1991 and our last in the summer of 1993; all but the last took place in my office in Rhinebeck; the final session occurred in London at the home of our editor Colin Chambers.

I first met David Jones in the spring of 1979 in the restaurant of the Gramercy Park Hotel in New York City. I was there to be interviewed for the part-time job of Literary Manager of the BAM Theatre Company that David was then forming at the Brooklyn Academy of Music. We hit it off OK and I got the job, which proved rather less enduring than our friendship and working relationship.

From that first meeting David was an influence on my writing. Specifically, he suggested I read Joseph Jefferson's nineteenth-century stage adaptation of *Rip Van Winkle*, thinking it might be a possible Christmas show for the company. Soon afterwards I began my own Rip Van Winkle play (which David would direct two years later). He also encouraged me to seek out lost American plays; this led not only to my continuing passion for such writers as George S. Kaufman and Ben Hecht, which engendered my own pastiche of American thirties' comedy *An American Comedy*, but also to the rediscovery by BAM of a number of American plays. From the day we met, David has guided and goaded me; his suggestions and reactions have had an effect upon my writing far greater than as the director of specific plays.

While at BAM, we worked for the first time together as writer and director. I wrote a new English language version of Brecht's *Jungle of Cities* which David directed. We worked on it during a time when BAM Theatre Company was collapsing, unable to meet its weekly payroll. As we worked, first on the script and then in rehearsal, David's great venture was folding around us. Our work on the play became our refuge from the painful knowledge of the company's imminent demise, a place of clarity and hope. There is nothing like adversity on which to build a lasting relationship.

A few months later, David directed his first play by me, *Rip Van Winkle or The Works*, at the Yale Repertory Theatre. It was four hours long, it had a cast of thirty, a flood, fire and a few battles and we nearly bankrupted the theatre. On opening night we looked at each other, reading each other's mind; if we could do this to ourselves and survive, we had a relationship that was going to last.

Our next play was *Principia Scriptoriae*, which David brought to the Royal Shakespeare Company and directed in 1986 in The Pit. *Between East and West* followed at the Hampstead Theatre, and *Sensibility and Sense* on television in America, *The End of a Sentence*, also on television, and *Misha's Party* (co-written with Gelman) which was produced by the RSC in The Pit. Through seven productions we have seen the best and the worst of each other; yet we are still friends and still want to work together.

Over fifteen years I have watched his children grow up; now he's watching mine. We've seen how our personal and private lives entwine with our work and inform it. We have influenced each other's thinking and beliefs. But I have never yet rehearsed a show with David where at least once I haven't wanted to stand up and say 'Just do it like I wrote it!' And I'm sure there hasn't been one show where David hasn't wanted to quote John Dexter: 'If you don't keep quiet, I'll direct it as you wrote it!'

Looking back over our conversations, I'm struck by how often we changed our minds. In one session I'd be arguing for X and in the next, against. I say how I hate to talk to actors. Two years later, the director can't shut me up. I can only explain this by saying that we change. As with all significant and long-standing relationships, change and the ability to change with our partners seem essential.

For a long time David and I referred to our book by its working title *Marriage or Divorce?* Throughout our discussions, you will see us struggling with the metaphor of the writer–director collaboration as a kind of marriage. And of course it is. The intensity and passion of this relationship are occasionally all-consuming; there have been years when I have had nearly as many meals with a particular director as with my wife. Such intensity, as in a marriage, breeds anxiety, jealousy, hate, passion, confusion, love, and finally – art.

RICHARD NELSON
Rhinebeck, New York, 1994

ONE Keats's Theory of Negative Capability: David Jones on Playwrights

> Shut up, Arnold, or I'll direct the play as you wrote it.
>
> *John Dexter to Arnold Wesker, on directing*
> Chicken Soup with Barley

RN: Let's start with a director's reasons for directing a particular play; what do you look for, what attracts you, what do you need from a new play?

DJ: It's a very gut reaction. The most important thing is, do you actually get a little *frisson* of excitement moment by moment as you read the play? You do not have to be able to necessarily visualize on the stage what you're reading on the page, but does the interaction of the characters, does what is said or what happens, really bring you up short and excite you? Is there an energy and a tension in the writing that is exciting you to want to put it up on its feet?

There is another thing – and I'm a little more suspicious of this as a motivation than I used to be. In the late sixties and seventies, I needed to feel that a play was about something, that it had something to say about society or about a way of life, an attitude of living. And I guess I still do subscribe to the Brechtian view that theatre is about the great art of living together. Therefore I wanted to do any play that seemed to me to add something to that store. That's a relic of a nonconformist up-bringing that one never quite gets rid of but I don't think that it's a bad motivation.

RN: What do you mean when you say the play should be about something?

DJ: I don't particularly like plays that reach conclusions. When I say a play is 'about' something, I want it to air certain problems, with great clarity and impact though without necessarily solving them, or to celebrate certain aspects of life, but leave a certain amount of work for the audience to do. I don't mean that you can take an easy moral away with you from having spent an evening in the theatre.

RN: But does it matter whether you agree with what it puts forward? If a play presents a point of view, need you subscribe to that point of view in order to direct it?

DJ: What one responds to may be more than content; it may be a tone of voice, which, OK, is modified into a number of various voices for the characters. There is a Shakespearean point of view or a Shakespearean style, although it varies enormously from play to play, but I find there is a commonality, just as I can pick up two pages of Richard Nelson and know Richard Nelson has written those two pages – which is not to say he's writing the same dialogue for each individual character, simply his consciousness informs the writing as a whole.

What is important is that there should be a sense of identification. To give a crass example; there is a long-windedness about Eugene O'Neill, whom I admire, which I find hard to come to grips with, a sense of going back over the ground and of repetition. I feel a bit of the same thing with Arthur Miller, although I admire him enormously too. My predilection is towards much more economical, terse, understated drop-a-small-pebble-in-the-lake-and-let-the-ripples-happen style of writing, like the way in which, say, Harold Pinter writes or you. Plays are exciting, however, when they look at familiar things from a new angle, showing you something in a way that is not the way you saw it before.

A very important element, also, is the large area covered by irony and humour. What I loved about David Mercer was that, however dark an area he was getting into, however confused a personal problem or however disillusioned or pessimistic a political point of view in the play, there was an enormous maverick sense of humour behind it.

So, I think you've got to sympathize with the playwright's tone of voice and the way that a playwright looks at the world in general. If there were a play which really had a point of view about the world or reached a moral conclusion which I found distasteful, I think I would find that difficult to do; but I can't honestly think of a play that I admired as a play but turned down for that reason.

RN: Let's stay with this a bit longer, with you, as a director, wishing to, hoping to, identify or sympathize with the tone of voice of the author. Let me give you an example – perhaps an extreme one – from my experience of working with Liviu Ciulei [leading postwar Romanian director who worked abroad in the 1970s, finally settling in America], who in time became not only my mentor but in many ways my artistic father. When you finally scratch the surface of what Liviu is doing in a production, very often he's trying to find out what one almost could say was his own archetypal story. He will move things around, directing, seeing things in such a way that it's his story that comes out of the text: Liviu's story is of a man who was chased out of his Romanian cultural environment by a barbarian – the Soviet system. So he sees the world always in clashes, between a culture and a barbarian, and everything he touches he looks at in that way.

There are times when I've seen your work and I've felt that you're really drawing from your life; there seem to be moments when you identify quite specifically, even personally, with the work. Is that a helpful way of approaching this or not?

DJ: I find that very difficult to answer. (*Pause.*) I don't know . . . (*Pause.*)

RN: Let me explain it another way; in this art form of directing, which is a form where you apparently take other people's work and you organize it, is there an element that is very personal and where you draw your creations and your organization from *your* past? Is that a fruitful way of growing in your work or does that lead to destruction?

DJ: I think that goes on unconsciously, perhaps. I never consciously pull a work in that direction. It touches on one of the big distinctions between doing a classic play and a modern one. With the latter hopefully you are trying to understand what it is that the playwright wants to say and how he or she wants it to be said. Yes, the script exists, but I do agree with Granville Barker that the script is a score awaiting a performance. Really it's a question of detective work and exploration and discovery, trying to find out what the animal is, and the playwright may not know initially when it's put on its feet what the animal's going to be. With the classics there's maybe more of a temptation (I sometimes think too much of a temptation) to say, 'What new slant can we put on this? How can we make this old story relevant now?' And that's when we get into conceptualized Shakespeare, for example. My main quarrel with that approach is that it is not conceptualized enough but usually a rag-bag of three or four smart-arsed ideas crammed onto a production rather than an attempt to find the inner heart of the play.

To this extent I don't think that I vary my approach from a classic to a new text. When I direct, say, *Pericles* or *As You Like It*, I'm not overtly concerned with whether I am doing it differently to how it was done before. I try to empty my mind of all the productions I've seen and go back to the script *au nature* again, as if it were a new play, to find out what I think the story wants to say. It's a little analogous (although this may be a bit high-flown) to a sculptor working on a piece of marble, for example. They say the trick is to allow the statue to come out of the block; that if you attack the marble with an absolutely set idea of what your Madonna and Child is going to be, then you will achieve a statue but it will have a certain deadness about it. There is something in the nature of that particular shape of stone you are working on which must be allowed to find its voice, and I think that is true of a play too.

RN: Just to pursue this point, can we take three examples from your work?: the English scenes in the film *84 Charing Cross Road* and, in my plays, the young and old character of Edward Chandler in *Sensibility and Sense* and the husband and wife in *Between East and West*. Watching you in rehearsal for the last two of those, it seems to me that your personal life, your own specific history, was brought to bear in directing the performances. I gather that, either in discussion with the actors or in terms of how you shot the English scenes in *84 Charing Cross Road*, you did the same there. Is that true?

DJ: That's interesting. It would never have occurred to me to have analysed it in that way but I think that you have picked three very good examples. The English scenes in the film are in a way profoundly personal, in that Frank Doel comes from a lower middle-class background of genteel poverty and my father was a Congregational minister, which gave my family a certain standing in the community but it meant we had no money in the bank whatsoever. So we were desperately trying to keep up a façade of respectability while living near the poverty line. The domestic life of the Doels – the meal at just such and such a time, and a very frugal meal – was something I knew about.

I lived through the war and rationing and that England is now completely lost and gone. It was an England which had a slightly naïve but very touching belief in goodness. It was England before the Fall but living in a time of austerity. Because that was the time of my childhood and adolescence I suppose I didn't feel nostalgically romantic about it. I just knew what it was like. I think Tony Hopkins, who is slightly younger than me but also has a Welsh background, knew exactly where Frank Doel as the 'Mr Ordinary' man-next-door came from. It's bizarre but Hugh Whitemore, who wrote the film, knew that generation too. He's also two or three years younger than me but we all knew what Britain was like during the war and, above all, just after. We had to invent more for the English scenes than we did for those with Helene Hanff, and in the initial lists of what Frank Doel might do at home Hugh had put 'cleaning shoes at night', which was a terribly English thing at that time. Somehow it never got into the script. Yet one day Tony said, 'I'd love to clean my shoes at some point, do you think you could find an opportunity?' I agreed. We didn't discuss it any more but we both knew that if he was given the chance to do that as the last thing before he went to bed it would say something about the character, and it's of great beauty what he does with that in the film. I didn't direct Tony on that scene; we just knew without saying what the scene was about. So, yes, that is personal, in the sense that a director says, 'I know this material, I've lived this. I'm not dangerously in love with it but I know it inside out.'

The piece in which I wasn't aware of it happening at all – but you were very close on this – was in *Sensibility and Sense*. I never for one moment thought of Edward as having a non-conformist minister father. There was something about the older Edward being caught in the cross-fire between two extremely powerful women that amused me, in particular in the way that he had learned to deal with the aggression of the second wife simply by stonewalling, keeping his head down and developing a wry sense of humour. I don't mean that it was autobiographical but I understood it. *Between East and West* was an interesting case, doubly so, because I was directing my wife as the wife of the director in the play, and both Sheila [Allen] and I had gone through the experience of exile and expatriation in America, obviously not with the same language problem that these two characters have but we did feel that . . .

RN: What was *your* language problem?

DJ: Well, not a *major* language problem but a language problem to the degree that after about nine or ten months in Brooklyn I realized that every sentence I spoke involved either a vocabulary or a pronunciation decision. I had a choice to make and I did start to stammer slightly, I mean only for a short period, and now I suppose I'm still making instant choices, depending on which country I'm in, but I'm not that aware of the schizophrenia.

I think Sheila and I both felt that the characters in your play could have been suggested by, or come out of some observation of, us trying to find our feet in Brooklyn, but I knew also that the play was much more profound and on the nerve-end closer, say, to the experience of Liviu and his wife's resettlement observed by you at first hand. I think there were lots of things in that play that I could understand and make funny, or make very simple things deeply touching – for example, the little scene with the wife where she's trying to do the language lesson. I tried never to invoke autobiography because I thought (I think rightly so) that that would have been very difficult for John Woodvine playing the director. I didn't really think then, and I don't think now, that the woman's Sheila and the man's me, but I do know about both the excitement and the terror of arriving and trying to remake your life in America.

RN: And visually you used images, such as the fire escapes that surrounded the set and the framed posters, which you associated with *your* first arrival in America.

DJ: Sure.

RN: If we can stay a little longer looking at the kind of work represented by these two plays of mine, *Sensibility and Sense* and *Between East and West*, and if we can take your interest in, and ability to direct, the work of Pinter, Gorky, Granville Barker – I don't know enough about David Mercer, but maybe you can comment later – then there does seem to be the basis of a very strong sub-textual feeder in your family background. And, I'll put words into your mouth, it's there in a double persona, your family 'putting up a front', where you had a social face as well as another world running behind it.

DJ: Absolutely.

RN: So, could you talk a little about this in relation to the plays that you've chosen to direct? Chosen perhaps not for what they say, which could relate to how you see the world, but more because through their perceptions or the way in which they deal with characters, they may have something to do with how you were brought up and how you see yourself.

DJ: Well, it's huge. I mean, that's seven years of analysis!

RN: (*Laughs.*)

DJ: Well ... I prefer complexity to directness – and the minute I say that, I immediately think that probably *84 Charing Cross Road* is one of the simplest stories that I've ever handled and I think that, in so far as I handled it well, it was because I was able to preserve its innocence and simplicity in a certain way.

I think that the most interesting human beings exist on many different levels; they have a public and a private persona and, if you're privileged, you can get to see their inner, creative/emotional side. Most people whom I have time for don't spread that around loosely; it is a privilege that you earn by becoming a friend or getting close to someone or being in love. Either for political or emotional reasons (if those two things are different) there are certain areas that have to be protected, there are certain lies that get told, there are certain camouflages that people move behind. That sort of richness of behaviour is fascinating to me.

On a personal level, in the handling of a rehearsal, for

example – and it is true of me but I think of every director – the director is either enormously two-faced, if you want to be pejorative, or certainly hidden in what his inner convictions or end-drives are going to be.

Curiously, I mistrust works which are too super-personal and private as well. I do like there to be an outer or social context of some sort for the story, but not necessarily a political point of view. What appeals to me about Gorky is that he presents an extraordinarily rich cross-section of a society, which just happens to be Russia, and it's a society at a moment of historical pressure and enormous imminent change and so everything is in a volatile state.

RN: And a great element of genteel poverty?

DJ: With Gorky? Well, no. The great difficulty with doing *The Lower Depths*, for instance, is that it isn't genteel poverty but hard, hard, hard, nose-in-the-grindstone poverty. It's one of the plays that I felt very humble about, in the sense that I don't know what it's like to be as poor as that. My background work was not, 'how did the Russian peasant live?'; it was, 'what does it mean to be poor?'

I think what you're poking away at is interesting. Perhaps more than I realize, I have been looking for a mirror in the material that I handle. I'm looking for a reliving or a reworking through certain areas and not just because they are familiar but also because my most important principle of work is Keats's theory of Negative Capability. When you are presented with an experience, and that experience can be a play or a new work, you empty yourself of preconceptions so that the work is allowed to take you over, to enter into your consciousness and somehow, at a certain point when you have absorbed it, you come to understand it. For Keats, at that point he could write the poem; for me, it's at that point that I can start to direct the play.

By definition we are talking about material that is quite often outside my ken and, as you know, the work I did on the first two or three Gorky plays was profoundly historical documentary in approach. I was pissed off with the fact that every English production of a Russian play, I thought, turned it into genteel middle-class England, and I didn't think that's what the plays were about. They were rawer than that; they had more animal energy. What I tried to find in them was something more dangerous, more physical, more non-intellectual than my up-bringing allowed me to be.

RN: Was that true for *Jungle of Cities* too?

DJ: *Jungle of Cities* bears little or no relation to anything that I have a personal history of. It's a totally invented America but that's interesting in itself. It's the myth of America as seen by Brecht. What I latched onto with *Jungle*, though, was the surrealism of those odd characters, like Baboon the pimp or Worm the hotel owner. I didn't understand what they meant. It was as if they came out of a fairy story and that appealed to me as just something to put up on the stage and it never struck me as being difficult.

The two words that used to panic me a lot when I was much younger were 'creative' and 'personal'. I knew I was critically sharp and could say why this was good and why that was bad but I didn't feel an upsurge of story-telling in myself. I felt I wasn't creative, but I could be interpretative, and it's a very fine line, as we know, between the two. I still prefer to think of a director and an actor as being primarily interpreters rather than creators.

The other thing that scared me was when people would say about essays I had written: 'It's extremely intelligent but I don't see where you stand.' This used to terrify me, because I thought I had no personal point of view.

I went to Cambridge extremely young when I was only seventeen. They were reluctant to take me that young but the army wouldn't accept me until I was eighteen – national service was still compulsory then – and I somehow managed to persuade the college to take me straight away. Everyone else on my course had done their national service so I was three years younger than them. If you read English at Cambridge, you take on a new author each week – so it's Keats one week, Graham Greene the next, George Eliot the week after. The way I dealt with that was very much the Keatsean thing of plunging myself into the author, searching for myself in the author and somehow coming out and distilling the author's point of view on the world.

I developed a chameleon personality through three very impressionable years, but at the end I had no idea what the fuck I thought about anything. What saved me was that I then had to go into the army, and I welcomed becoming almost a cipher for the best part of six months, during basic training. Then, during my twentieth year, slowly and painfully and tentatively and insecurely I began to arrive at certain points of view.

Interestingly, some of the best reviews I've had, or the comments that have pleased me most about my work, say that my direction is invisible, that it is as if *the* story, *the* play has been allowed to come through and be totally expressed, and you're not aware that it has been directed. That's a very different school of direction to where the director wants you to know that he is the director, because he wants to add something to the story. In my view, directing is not so much adding to the story as trying to find out what the maximum potential of the story is and allowing that to be expressed, for the story to tell itself without undue interference.

*

Brecht was very, very tiresome today until (I'm sorry to say) I was stern and a trifle shitty. Then he behaved.

Orson Welles on working with Bertolt Brecht on Galileo

RN: Now, to push this one step farther, as we are provisionally calling this book *Marriage or Divorce?*, before marriage there's falling in love. Well, there's a way of falling in love with an object in which that object fills a need; it's something that you are not, or that you wish to be.

DJ: Right.

RN: And then there's seeing yourself in the object, seeing your reflection, your own thoughts articulated. I think directors can experience both, perhaps in different degrees with different directors.

DJ: I think it's in the middle of those two extremes. Both those things can happen. There can be an energy or a vigour or a kind of abandon about something theatrical which is not part of your temperament, but you wish it were, and you can respond enormously to that. That's the attraction of opposites, I guess. I would be much more dubious about the contrary – and I'd like to think I'm tough on it – if I see in a play that there is a mirror image of my personality or my background. I'm much more attracted by something different to me than something totally similar.

You really fall in love when you read a play and think that this writer understands the secrets of the human heart, that they know those little moments that people don't admit to or that are really the centre of a relationship, that this person is on your wavelength and you can appreciate what they're talking about. It's a sense of sharing, of shared insight.

I know this was the case with David Mercer [leading English stage and television playwright, 1928–80], and I don't think I've ever felt it quite the same with anyone else. He was a totally different man from me. He was five years older, he was very North Country, he had a major drinking problem. He was like a roaring bear of a man. But when I picked up a page of his dialogue I felt he wrote like I would have if I had been a playwright. He was saying all the things I felt and yet he came from quite a different background. I can't explain this, but it felt as if it were my voice on the page.

RN: Just talk about that – what that voice is that you felt – that's a really hard one, I know.

DJ: (*Long pause.*) It was a very caring voice, but it had a particular wry sense of humour that was very often self-mocking. The central character in a Mercer play is often very funny, but in a slightly destructive way in that he or she is nearly always a profound idealist who has become cynical. Mercer expresses the cynicism with a pith and an energy that can take you beyond it into even a positive frame of mind.

David was often a depressive character; very astute in his political analysis of the world and very depressed by the fact that the major socialist experiment of Eastern Europe had not worked in the ways that he wished. He would not pretend that it was otherwise and therefore he became a kind of outsider within the militant left, which is where he belonged. He could walk dialectic rings around the Socialist Labour League boys who were on the Trotskyite bandwagon and who saw David as selling out.

He focused and sharpened in me a political awareness that had been very generalized, decent liberal before. I think he made me more mature politically, though what appealed to me about him was the detachment of his stance, that he was totally for the Marxist ideal even though he felt that the Marxist experiment had not worked in practice.

He was quite a clumsy writer in a curious way, or seemed to be clumsy. I'll never forget the first reading of *Belcher's Luck* – I thought, none of this works, and the actors could not get their tongues around the sentences. And then after about two weeks I realized what he was doing; I said, this dialogue is like very heavy telegraph poles – once you find the point of balance, you can do anything you want with it. You had to get it up in the air and away.

Mercer's work is not the filed down minimalist statement akin to poetry that Harold Pinter's writing is. I always loved the fact that Harold had enormous admiration for David, more for the man he was and the attitude he stood for than because he was a particular sort of writer. Stylistically, they were poles apart, but they had a sympathy for each other as people.

I may have projected certain things into my relationship with David which were not entirely there ... I don't know, but it was *the first*, and to me, therefore, probably *the most* important, ongoing relationship I had with a writer.

RN: Tell me about meeting David Mercer for the first time. There are two different questions here: one is about meeting the writer for the very first time and the other, as with Mercer, is about the first meeting to discuss a new play after you've already established a relationship over a number of plays.

DJ: Hard to remember the first time. I did a small play of David's that ran about fifty minutes called *The Governor's Lady*. It was part of an evening of one-act plays at the Aldwych called *Expeditions One*, which was a way of doing new writing and encouraging people who hadn't done anything major. It was a play which had been commissioned for radio and then turned down by the controller of the Third Programme because it was too obscene, but we managed to get it past the Lord Chamberlain with a few changes here and there.

David was already one of the leading television playwrights in England – if not *the* one – and he'd only had one stage play done, in Manchester. But the stage to him – and it remained so – was the area in which he most wanted to succeed and the one in which he always felt, I think wrongly, a slight sense of inadequacy. He was never quite sure if he wrote well for the stage, whereas writing for television, which in some ways in terms of innovation was much more difficult, never struck him as being a problem.

So what I remember was that I had on my hands an enormously grateful writer, because a play that had just been banned was about to be done and it was being done on stage.

RN: What was the process when David wrote a play? Did he send it to you or did he send it to the RSC?

DJ: I don't think we commissioned David . . . I'm trying to remember. Quite often David would say, 'I really feel like doing a new play for the stage. I want to talk to you about the ideas I've got.' We'd have a business lunch and it's my belief that David didn't really begin to think about the play until he sat down opposite me. He improvised brilliantly in his cups and he would come up with a kind of synopsis out of nowhere, which was not carefully prepared or studied. I think he sometimes had a germ . . . and then he'd go off and write it.

With *After Haggerty* he just had this idea of a crazy black power activist who was not in the play but sent telegrams to this rather effete English drama critic with left-wing tendencies who'd sold out.

RN: And what did you do? You just listened?

DJ: What he wanted was a sounding board. Occasionally I'd say, 'That sounds good,' or, 'That sounds dubious,' or, 'That's really exciting,' or, 'That sounds like a hell of a character.' David was like a lot of writers. He could be a work evader, you know. I think he needed to have that meeting, to have spoken about something to that point, so that he then had to put his talent where his mouth had been, and then go off and start to write the thing.

Although people think of David Mercer alongside Harold Pinter as one of the great ongoing writer–company relationships, I had a battle of one sort or another to get every play of David's on at the RSC. There was some debate on *The Governor's Lady*, for example: was this sailing too close to the wind? It's about the widow of a retired colonial governor, and in her fantasy life he comes back as a gorilla and ravishes her under a mosquito net. It's hilariously funny, but some people thought it was in poor taste.

With *Belcher's Luck* I don't think there was any question

about us doing it, but I do remember very clearly Peter Hall [then RSC artistic director] coming to a final run-through in Stratford and saying, 'There's nothing I can say to help you. I think this show is a total disaster. The play is clumsy and pretentious and I don't think you've begun to solve it and I don't know how you can do it. Sorry.'

This may have been cleverer than I realized, in that it made me *so* mad that I thought, 'Fuck it, I believe in this play and this play can be done and, shit, this is just a run-through.' I really worked on it and Peter did have the grace when he saw it in the theatre to say, 'I don't know what you did in the last ten days, but it's transformed.' But he was always a little uncertain about David's talent.

David then wrote what I think was his best stage play, *After Haggerty*, which not only had a very good run at the Aldwych but we transferred it to the West End for a very successful six months – the first RSC new play to do so. Peter Hall and the Planning Committee had wanted to turn this play down. I just couldn't believe it. They didn't think it was very funny and they didn't understand what the play was about.

David was distraught because he regarded the Royal Shakespeare as family. He said, 'I need a home. I need the security of feeling that I can take my work to this place and, all things being equal, it will get done.' He knew, as I knew, that this was probably his best piece of work. Harold Pinter was marvellous on this occasion. I rang him and said, 'Harold, I'm at my wit's end. Would you read this play because I think it's a great play?' He said, 'I don't even need to read the play. It's a disgrace that the RSC are not doing it.' He did in the end read the play and agreed that it was a terrific play, the best one David had written so far, and he wrote to Peter and said, 'You will be perpetually ashamed if you turn your back on this writer. You *have* to do this play.' Peter acquiesced but said it was on my head, so I was carrying the can.

I went into a much more dangerous situation with David's next play, *Duck Song*. It's a very strange, innovative work that nobody really quite got at the time, but which Alain Resnais was so inspired by that he got David to write the movie *Providence* for him out of it. I think that *Duck Song* was a commission, though David didn't want the money as much as to know that it would be done. He had only written one act of the play at the point when we had to announce that we were going to do it. He had a bad writing block on it and it was at a time when his drinking problem was at its most extreme.

This raised the issue of company loyalty to a writer, which was very important on that occasion. You know how important it is to a writer's security and confidence to know that there is a home that believes in you as a writer.

On *Duck Song*, it came down to a personal friendship. I didn't know if David was going to be able to complete this play, I didn't know if it was going to be the worst play ever written, but I was going to state my belief in his talent on the basis that somehow I could hold his hand through this period and we would arrive at something together. That's the two levels of loyalty – there's a kind of public and a private loyalty. With David I went through most of the demands – demands is the wrong word – but most of the closeness that I think should happen between a director and a writer.

David could be lazy, he could be obtuse, he could have real blockage. Because we were temperamentally very different, I could always cajole him with a certain amount of humour. He liked to feel the 'bad boy' and feel guilty and, although I was younger than him, I could play the school prefect and tell him to get himself in shape.

RN: Let's continue with first meetings. What happened with Graham Greene when you first met to talk about *The Return of A. J. Raffles*?

DJ: My first meeting with Greene was actually an audition, though I didn't realize until halfway through. I can't remember how the play came to be presented to the RSC, but I think that Ron Bryden, who was then the literary manager, was probably the first person to be enthusiastic about it. We were having a very tough time at the Aldwych, forced almost to doing ad hoc productions, but trying to keep a Royal Shakespeare repertoire spirit going.

I read the play and it excited me both as the Artistic Director of the Aldwych and as a director as such. Ron was very clever because he never said Graham was exercised about who directed the play. All he said was that Graham would love us to come down to Brighton and have lunch with him.

We met in a little pub called The Cricketers. Graham was a very British kind of gent, rather shy and he stammered a little bit to start with. We began to talk about the play rather stiffly and then I went off to the lavatory. When I came back the atmosphere seemed much more relaxed. We had a great lunch and afterwards Ron said, 'It's going to be all right.' I said, 'What do you mean? What's going to be all right?' Ron replied, 'He likes you.' 'Was this the problem?' I asked innocently. 'Oh yes,' said Ron, 'I wasn't sure until you went out to the gents and Graham said, "I think he'll do."'

As I remember, Graham had to go back to France. I don't think I involved him that closely with casting. It was a marvellous, strong cast: Paul Rogers, Denholm Elliott, Clive Francis, Peter Blythe, Gordon Gostelow, Michael Bryant; those were all names that he took on trust rather than sitting in auditions with me. It was kind of old-fashioned, but I felt that Graham was extremely anxious about whether we were going to do the play properly yet felt that it wasn't any part of his job to interfere, other than when he was asked to.

I think he came to the early read-through of the play and then to the first run-through and he had useful comments but never a great deal of input. I think he found the atmosphere so unlike what he had been used to that he just sat back and enjoyed himself in rehearsal.

RN: What we've been talking about with Greene is really a

director's relationship to a play. Let's take another play-wright, like John Arden, where the relationship becomes something else. This is the writer of the play you want to do, and what that person is, who he is, how he functions, becomes a new element in the 'marriage'.

DJ: You've again picked another instance where the first meeting was an audition – much more intensive, much more prolonged, and it was a double audition of myself and Timothy O'Brien who was going to design the show. Again, neither of us thought there was any question about whether we were doing the show or not when we went to the meeting.

It was a very bold choice to take on *The Island of the Mighty*. It had been around for a little bit and nobody really knew how to handle it because it was this mammoth trilogy. There had been some talk of doing it on three nights. I had made it clear, however, purely by correspondence and maybe through Peggy Ramsay, John Arden's and Margaretta D'Arcy's agent, that we were prepared to do a blockbuster evening but it was to be a single evening, if he and Margaretta were prepared to prune the plays down. That had been agreed until I went out to Ireland with Tim to meet them in Connemara, believing we were going to our first working meeting to exchange views on how they saw the play and its presentation – in fact to get their input and consult with them as to how they thought the whole thing should happen.

We spent a weekend there. We were picked up and they said, 'We want to drive you out to somewhere very remote because we've got a lot of difficult things to talk about.' And they did, indeed, drive us out almost to the tip of Connemara and sat us down on the beach and we were grilled remorse-lessly for about two and a half hours about our political attitudes, particularly to the presence of the British in Ireland, to the Marxist ethic and to working for a 'totalitarian' 'establish-ment' organization like the Royal Shakespeare Company. It was very difficult to get around to talking about the play.

RN: Was this a shock or did you expect this?

DJ: It was quite a shock. I knew that they would have very particular ideas. It's such an original, strange piece of work and it's a very political piece of work. I didn't have any problem with the politics in any sense and I thought that should John Arden know a little bit more about me, he would have no problem with me. I had by then directed *The Plebeians Rehearse the Uprising* [by Günther Grass], *The Silver Tassie* [by Sean O'Casey] and *Enemies* [by Maxim Gorky]. I would say in terms of their political stance and their protest about certain things these plays would make it very clear that what John was interested in exploring was something that I would be interested in exploring. But I was taken aback and then very amused by it – which I didn't show – then I thought, well fine, if that's what they really need to find out. Tim, I think, was much more shaken by it than I.

By the end of the meeting it all seemed to be fine. They said, 'Tomorrow we'll start to talk about the play but first we want you to be a part of this eviction demonstration we're organizing in the morning. We need you to come to this pub in Oughterard. The guys that run the pub and some of the people there are the villains behind this eviction that we're fighting.'

It was an eviction of a family from a cottage that they were taking a very strong public stance about. And they said, 'It could be very dangerous. Are you prepared for physical violence?' I said, 'Yes, if this is helpful to you. We'll be there.' For a while Tim didn't want to go at all but we turned up and it was a perfectly normal Sunday lunchtime in an Irish pub. We got a few looks, but it was actually a very up-market pub.

We sat there for about an hour and Margaretta was very conspiratorial about it. She kept going off and talking in corners to little huddles of people and then coming back. And then we walked out and she said, 'Well that was great. That really scared them.' I said, 'I'm sorry?' She said, 'Well, just your presence there. They think you're reporters from the *Sunday Times*, and this is what I spread around, so they know they're really in trouble now. They know that the heavy people turned up.'

I thought this was all a little bit fantasy-land but, fine. And then she said, 'Why don't you go back to the island and start to talk about the play?' We got into this small boat and went out to this little island where they lived. We had a terrific meeting for about an hour and a half – just John and myself and Tim – where we did talk about the need to cut and John talked about the way he saw the play visually. He described these marvellous Celtic backdrops and said that he wanted the scene setting to be done by images rather than by 3-D physicality. This was a very interesting idea and we got a long way exploring this, and we talked some casting ideas. This was a really *good* first meeting with the author.

At this point, Margaretta and some friends came back from the mainland and everything was very cheery and she asked if we'd had a good talk with John. I said, 'Yeah, great. We just had a little walk around the island and we're about to explore it.' The island was about a mile long and it was a lyrical afternoon and Tim and I went and sat on a rock. Tim was beaming but I had this sudden premonition, a sense that we were missing a move and I said, 'Tim, I think we have to get back. I think we have to get back to that cottage *now*!' He said, 'I don't understand,' and all I said was, 'Just believe me.'

We walked back to the house and opened the door, and the table had been rearranged to face the door. Sitting behind it, like in a court-martial, waiting for us to return were Margaretta and John and two friends. There were two chairs set in front. Margaretta said, 'I'm very distressed by the way you've been talking to John about the play and I think John said some things about it he should not have said, and I want you to sit down and we're going to tell you how this thing has to be done.'

We were right back to square one again, but this time it was more artistic; 'You have absolutely no right to cut any part of this play and we are going to run it in full.' I said, 'This is not the deal. The deal is, we have to get it into a manageable evening. And a manageable evening may turn out to be four and a half hours, but it is *one* evening.' We fought the case, but the attitude again had become very inquisitorial and there was still a sense that they were not convinced that we were the right people to do the play. Yet, by the end, I felt very secure about the foundation that we had built with John.

We discussed rehearsals and very much to my surprise Margaretta said, 'I don't think I should be involved at all – I really think John should be there from the beginning, but I don't know if you will object to that.' I said, 'Absolutely not, I want him to be there.' It was agreed that John would be there from the start. Margaretta said that maybe she would come over for three weeks. We left the next morning.

Then I got this letter. During our trip we had driven in Tim's Land-Rover somewhere. Tim was talking about his visit to Afghanistan which John was very interested in. While driving, Tim started to drive on the wrong side of the road because he was thinking and talking about Afghanistan and a car came around the corner and we had a slightly narrow shave. Nothing more was said, except I saw that Margaretta looked a bit rattled.

This letter said that the talks had been productive but she and John felt that Timothy O'Brien was an unsuitable choice to design this play; first, because he was the son of an Indian army family, and this was not the sort of background that was going to help him understand the play, and secondly, they felt that he had deliberately endangered John's life while in Ireland.

At this point, you realize you are moving into an area of high personal fantasy. I wrote back and said I was sorry but I could not accept this. Tim was the chosen designer and Tim was designing this show and that was that. There was no discussion about it and nothing more was said. Tim worked very lovingly and, I thought, very brilliantly on the set and every moment of its development was presented to John and got his approval. When Margaretta came over, it was one of her main objections that she hated the set, but without much chapter and verse being given for why.

So that was the first encounter with John Arden and I remember very vividly coming back and saying to Trevor Nunn [then RSC artistic director], 'I have to report to you this series of events. I'm calm about this. I love this play. I think it's very tough to do and it's going to be doubly tough because I think we're going to have our problems with the authors but I don't foresee major difficulties with John. He's going to be there all the time. But you should know, I think, we're moving into a potential risk area.' For five weeks it went smoothly and I'd been wrong in my fears. Then – then I was proved right. *The Island of the Mighty* opened at the RSC's Aldwych Theatre in December 1972. The authors picketed preview performances as a protest against the production.

RN: In this case, or in other cases, did you spend time talking to other people about the writer before the first meeting? Did you try to contact other directors who had worked with John?

DJ: No, I didn't. It's curious but I'll do that sometimes when I'm working with an actor I've never worked with before and I'm not sure whether to cast. I do it much more if I'm working with a new stage manager or someone like that. With writers, on the whole, I've wanted to find out for myself . . . and I've wanted to go in without preconceptions. People are extraordinarily different with different people and I might get a false lead on a writer's personality, quirks, or idiosyncrasies from another director.

RN: Continuing with first meetings . . .

DJ: My first meeting with Harold Pinter was fascinating

because I was working as an actor with a big amateur theatre group in north London called The Tavistock Repertory. I was in the third ever production of *The Birthday Party*. The first had run for exactly one week in London and the play then had a very short run in Scarborough.

Harold came to the Tavistock because he was still unsure whether he was a playwright or not. With the exception of Harold Hobson, everyone else had said this is trash, this is nonsense, this play means nothing. So he came to rehearsals with great enthusiasm. I was playing McCann, the psychotic Irishman, and the actor playing Goldberg, the other part of the invasive duo, was in another show and quite often couldn't come to rehearsal. Harold would step up and read Goldberg.

So my first experience of Harold was hearing the author as actor saying the lines out loud. Doing those inquisitorial double-act scenes was just extraordinary. I learned what the Pinter rhythm was as an actor on the rehearsal floor.

The next time I met him was when we featured *The Caretaker* in the television arts programme *Monitor* for which I shot several scenes from it and Huw Weldon did a major interview with him. And then, as I arrived at the RSC, Harold was becoming the RSC's primary house dramatist with *The Homecoming*. When *Landscape* and *Silence* were being set up, I became a go-between man between Peter Hall and Harold, and I had to find out from Harold what his casting ideas were.

RN: Why?

DJ: I think Peter was busy doing something else at the time. I was called the artistic controller and Peter's view of this was that he was the commanding officer and I was his adjutant. He would make global artistic decisions and then I would run around and see that they were carried out. If he decided to do a play, I might go and do some research on it.

With *Landscape* and *Silence* Harold was characteristically unforthcoming in that the characters are not exactly described. I said, 'When we start to think about casting the woman, how old do you think?' And he said, 'It's really very hard to say from the text. I guess she could be anything between twenty-two and about forty.' I said, 'Do you think she's fair or dark?' And he said, 'I don't think there's anything in the play that tells us that.' And I said, 'Aha,' but he said, 'No, really, it's a mystery to me who this woman is.'

It was not done with a great deal of mischief. It was as if this character had emerged from his head onto the page, but the outlines of this character were still very indeterminate. He suggested that maybe the most helpful thing was to start naming some actresses and he would tell me whether they might fall into the ball park of what's going on there.

It was very similar to something he said to me when I was playing McCann. I'd said 'I don't quite understand how the duo arrived in Brighton' and he replied, 'I can't tell you anything about that. I know nothing about these people other than what they do in the room. Don't ask me anything about their background, where they come from, how much money they earn, what they eat. Anything I know about them is in the play. I can't tell you more than that.'

This was regarded as startling dramaturgy in those days. But, of course, it is exactly the way you encounter people in life, until you get to know people well. What you know is what comes through the door and what you deal with from clues you then get. Other dramatists might say, 'That's what I want to present on the stage, but I can give you the background history. I can tell you what the bottom of the iceberg is.' Harold will never mess with that. He will not answer questions on that.

TWO

Close to Death:
Richard Nelson on Directors

> When it was Sunday and Jed [Harris, director of *The Crucible*] said it was Tuesday and you corrected him, he would grin mischievously with his heavy lower jaw jutting forward and say 'I never argue with talent.'
>
> *Arthur Miller*

DJ: Insofar as you have ever been free to pick a director, or insofar as you look for a talent that you think would understand your work and do it well, what do you look for? How do you 'director spot'?

RN: It's very difficult. It's almost impossible to 'director spot'. I think that if you admire a certain kind of work or if you admire a production, then you may want to meet that director. But it's an odd relationship when you begin because someone has come to you and, if they're clever, then the director has said, 'I love your play.'

DJ: I want your body.

RN: Exactly. I want your child and I want to take the child off and make this child grow. So you love that person for doing that. The tricky thing for a playwright, I think, is to keep some distance at that point and to *not* listen.

DJ: Not be over-grateful.

RN: That's the word. And it's very hard. It's taken me a long time to develop my own rules. What you said about Pinter was very interesting. It is very good just to be able to say 'This is all I know and I wrote it and now let's figure out what this person wrote.' It's a nice way of dealing with the problem, but I'm not sure that everyone is emotionally capable of dealing with it that way.

With my work, there are certain kinds of things that I look for. I think of my work as very clean.

DJ: By 'clean' do you mean hard-edged or are you talking more of maturity?

RN: No. Hard-edged, clean, in a visual way, in a rhythmic way. I work a lot on where something begins, where something ends. How much fits in a real world, how much doesn't fit in a real world, how much is theatrical, how much is not. All these things I play with a lot and so need someone who has developed these same senses, these same concerns at least to the extent that I have. Otherwise, and I've certainly been in this situation, you feel like you're educating someone and then the kind of responses and comments that you get from a director can be completely destructive because they have not understood your play.

DJ: You quizzed me as to whether I fell in love with material because – to put it in very banal terms – it was the story of my life or because it was complementary, something totally different from what I knew. For you, it is crucial that a director really understands what it is you have written and how you want the story to be told. Is it better, therefore, if a director is very much in tune with your work and similar in personality to you, or do you think there's a positive benefit from having someone who says, 'I don't see things quite like that'?

RN: I think the best directors for my work are people who have gone on similar journeys to mine. So I do think that there is a sympathy and an understanding that's necessary.

DJ: You're talking about life journeys and living through certain political attitudes.

RN: Yeah, I think so.

DJ: Or emotional beliefs?

RN: Both ... both ... I'd say more so emotional beliefs, or life problems. Thematically, there is a great concern in my work with where art fits into life and I have always gravitated towards directors who have this concern as well, and vice versa.

DJ: To believe that art does have something to say about the way in which you conduct your life?

RN: Yes, but also in more complicated ways – watching how art can be an escape, an enjoyable escape, sometimes in the conscious awareness of, or feelings of guilt about, such an escape.

I find that the directors whom I've worked with best also seem to be very intelligent and interested in words and the patterns I create. When I've dealt with someone like André Serban [Romanian director who has spent most of his career in America and Western Europe], who is very intelligent, visually brilliant, but not that interested in language, I've felt great, great frustration. But each relationship is unique – there is simply the difference between who a director and a writer is, their personalities.

DJ: Very true.

RN: As you know, for example, I don't particularly enjoy talking to actors about my work, unlike a director. And when I have talked, sometimes I've been incredibly confusing.

DJ: Yes, and you are also quite wickedly amused sometimes at watching the director try to talk. (*Laughter*.)

You had quite a variety of youngish American directors with your early work. Did you have a strong concept of what the director–writer relationship should be? What did you expect from the director and were you very disillusioned or were you excited?

RN: I was pretty disillusioned. I felt that by and large these younger directors didn't know what to make of a playwright–director relationship. They really felt the need to have an input in the material – a very specific input – and they judged success or even their job by how much a director influenced the work. That left the playwright, me, in a number of peculiar positions.

I finally worked out after some difficult times, including walking out on a production in Los Angeles, what a director's domain is and what a playwright's domain is. How a director stages a play is the director's domain. The only thing I demand, and I believe it is my right, is to spend enough time with the director, whenever or in whatever way the director wishes, until I am convinced that he or she understands my intentions.

If they wish not to follow those intentions in ways that I don't understand, so be it. That's their job. That's their domain. But if I feel that the play's intentions are not being understood, or that the director does not wish to spend time trying to deal with or understand those intentions, then I am completely lost and frustrated.

DJ: I can see that. Then you're excluded and you are being denied access to your 'child'. How often have you been able to choose your director?

RN: In most cases I've been in a position of being able to approve a director. So I don't actually choose, but I could prevent. And I have said 'no' numerous times.

DJ: Now that's fascinating. Have you said 'no' because it's someone who has fucked up your work before, or it's someone whose work you've seen and can't subscribe to, or is it because of things you've heard from fellow writers?

RN: Mostly it's because of work I've seen. If I don't see that cleanness, or if I don't see a certain sympathy . . . if the person has done, let's say, twelve musicals in a summer stock playhouse and six Neil Simon plays, I don't understand why that person is being asked to direct my play. I'll meet with that person, but I'll be very suspicious at the beginning of the meeting.

I have had situations where I've interviewed directors but I confess to not knowing what I'm interviewing for. You're maybe getting a feel. A couple of times I've said 'no' to directors simply because I met them and they seemed extraordinarily bored. I've thought, 'I don't want to sit in the rehearsal room with someone who is bored with things.'

DJ: Right.

RN: Maybe this is simply a way of being shy that comes off as boredom.

DJ: But they come off as bored with life in general . . .

RN: As if they've been on the circuit doing one show after another and they'll fit in mine between going to St Louis and Cincinnati.

But there's different ways of finding out about the situation. Once years ago a director and I met to discuss his directing a production of an early play of mine called *Jungle Coup*. The play was about a reporter who gets lost in a jungle, and slowly the jungle becomes a theatre and the reporter begins to speak directly to the audience. The director liked the play and I had liked a few productions of his and so we agreed to meet. The first thing he said to me was, 'I want to do an environmental set.' I was surprised by this. I said to him that the whole dynamic of the play was the breaking down of the 'fourth wall', and if there wasn't a fourth wall to break down, then I didn't understand how the play could work. He said he understood that, but that he'd never done a show with an environmental set, and as that was what he wanted to do next, it was either going to be my show or someone else's. Let's say we agreed to disagree and he never directed the show.

In another production of another play of mine, the producer and I were desperately looking for a director; a show in the theatre's season had been cancelled and mine had suddenly been pushed forward. Finally, I suggested that the producer, who was also a well-known director, direct it. I'd spent time with the producer on this search and thought it was an interesting idea. The producer was surprised when I asked, and asked for a night to think it over, then called back the next day to say, 'Yes, I'd love to.' I replied, 'Oh, great!' but in the next breath the producer said, 'I just want to tell you that I happen to think Ronald Reagan is a really good president, and I believe in most of the things he's doing. I just wanted you to understand that before we begin.'

DJ: (*Laughter.*) Did the production go ahead?

RN: The production went ahead. I didn't stop it, but that little announcement devastated me. The play is very political and is about a politician.

DJ: But did the production end up as a Reaganite production?

RN: No. I don't think it had any political thrust at all. It was sort of neutral, reflecting, I think, the confusion of our relationship. If only the order of our conversation had been reversed, if the director had said, 'This is what I believe. Now I'm not sure if we're sympathetic,' then I would have said, 'You're right, we're not.' Or, 'Let's talk about it as it relates to the play.' But as I had just expressed joy that the producer had agreed to direct my play, I felt there was no room to discuss what the producer then told me.

*

> Well, dear Anton Pavlovich, we played *Uncle Vanya*. You will see from the reviews, probably, we didn't manage to cover up some of the faults of the play . . . [There was] a certain theatrical slowness over $2\frac{1}{2}$ acts, despite the fact that we cut 40 of the 50 pauses you ask for. We cut them little by little during rehearsals.
>
> *Nemirovich-Danchenko to Chekhov, in a letter*

DJ: One of the great solaces to a director is working with a writer who will share the trials and tribulations of the rehearsal at the end of the day.

RN: I think that there's a lot of directors who wouldn't understand that.

DJ: Or wouldn't want that.

RN: If you're going to have your input to a director, you need to find the least threatening time – the time that can be seen as having the least other meanings – which is a social time, a relaxed time. Still, some directors feel there's a need to take on all the burden and others feel that if they discuss with the playwright it'll just open a door to more complaints – I'm sure there are also playwrights like this.

DJ: If you're in a destructive situation then I guess it continues along those lines. But it seems to me you have got three, maybe four, directors who have proved they know quite a bit about your work and handle it well. It would be invidious to make any comparisons, but as you write a new work, how do you choose which one to go to? Is that to do primarily with availability or do you know the right people for the right plays?

RN: It's hard. I think that it's probably every writer's dream or ambition to work well with one particular director. You see those few relationships that have existed through the years, and you can be very envious of them.

The directors you're talking about in relation to me are people who have careers that span a lot of different ambitions and therefore it was clear to me a number of years ago that no director of that kind of stature and talent could consistently do all my work. Also I write a great deal.

DJ: I was going to say you're prolific so the plays are coming off the assembly line at a rate and it's crucial you have more than one avenue to pursue. But do you think that you will reach a point where director A in your view might be wrong for play B and director C would be much better for it?

RN: It's not so much a question of one director not being suitable, it's more that sometimes you do get on rolls with people where one play fits into another play and the shorthand of one play fits into an understanding of another. There was a tie for you and I between *Principia* and *Sensibility*. There's also a tie between *Some Americans Abroad* and *Two Shakespearean Actors* in the sense that they are both very much plays about a contained community, an insular community.

One thing that Roger Michell showed me with his direction of *Some Americans* was his profound understanding of an essentially tight little community. I think – and this goes back to what we were talking about with a director's background – it has to do with Roger being sent to boarding school when he was very young. In a boarding school, very small gestures . . .

DJ: You can't evade the group . . .

RN: How the group functions through tiny gestures is in your blood. So, there's being on a roll, and then the director has to be available, and want to do it.

The plays match the director in some ways or they work out matching because of the nature of the director. For example, I would be very cautious of doing a new play with someone like Liviu, whom I admire profoundly. I would want to sit down and make sure that he knew it wasn't a blueprint for *his* play.

DJ: I understand.

RN: My relationship with Liviu was very clear from our first meeting when I had been hired to do a translation/adaptation of Molière's *Don Juan* for Arena Stage [Washington, DC]. Liviu was in Romania at the time; therefore, I had to do an adaptation without a single briefing or meeting with him. All anyone knew was that he wanted to set it in the late nineteenth century and so, on the basis of that, I did some research and found out some reasons why I thought he might want to set it then, which were all the wrong reasons as it turned out.

We finally met in his hotel room in New York City after I'd written a draft and when we began it was very clear that he was troubled by what he had in front of him. I couldn't get him to articulate what was wrong, so we sat down with the script; he had the French text, a Romanian translation, my script and a number of other texts, and we went through my version word by word. After the first day we had worked on one page, changing virtually every word to the point where I thought what we had was absolutely unreadable let alone playable. It was a complete mess that made no sense and that seemed to read like an awkward, a terrible translation from the Romanian.

So we continued. By about halfway through the second page I kept trying to quit because I thought the whole thing was a disaster. This man was giving me no respect: maybe I had a slight facility with the English language that was a little bit better than Liviu's and that was the only need for Richard Nelson, it seemed. And if only Liviu had a little more time and practice to work on his English then there wouldn't be any need for me. I was obviously wrong about that, but that's how it felt.

Then we got to a point where we were yelling at each other over the translation of three words: '*Il faut que*'. Sganarelle says '*Il faut que* Don Juan burns in hell.' You can translate this '*il faut que*' as 'it is necessary' that Don Juan burns in hell, meaning Sganarelle thinks that it had better happen or it must happen that this man burns in hell. In other words it is a moral cry. Or this '*il faut que*' can be translated as 'it's bound to happen', meaning . . .

DJ: It's inevitable.

RN: Yes. That it's the way of the world. We can't do anything about it. So one is a relationship between a master and a servant where the servant wants the master to die, and the other is a surrender to the world – there's nothing we can do and the world just goes on about us and we take our fate. My interest in the play had been the first one – a very dynamic relationship between Sganarelle and Don Juan – and it was very, very clear that Liviu's was the second.

Finally, after three or four hours of sorting out this dilemma, I said, 'OK. It's a completely different way of doing this adaptation. I'll do it, but here's the deal. Now I understand why you were criticizing those other words and now I know how to make them work in a different way. But now you have to leave me alone, and I'll deliver the script.'

DJ: But did that realization of the totally opposing views explain what might have seemed like only pedantry on Liviu's part?

RN: Absolutely, because the whole first page is a speech of Sganarelle's. It's about Sganarelle being angry and so the energy was very harsh, coming from a servant who hated and was trapped by a way of life where you had to be duplicitous.

Whereas Liviu's version was, 'Oh, *c'est la vie*.' That's the way life is. Isn't this amazing how life turns out. You can imagine the rhythm is everything. Anytime there was a choice, which was every word, it was a different choice. So what happened? Well, Liviu trusted me, and I went away and rewrote the whole thing quite quickly with this whole different kind of rhythm.

DJ: Right.

RN: I presented it to Liviu and he made a few changes here and there – very tiny changes – and then it went into rehearsal and very little was changed during rehearsal.

DJ: It's interesting that the first really one-to-one director–writer relationship you and I had was doing an adaptation, of *Jungle of Cities*. I may have a rosy view of this, but the fact that we were working on something which didn't belong to either of us freed us to talk about language and theatricality. I learned more about where you were coming from and what you found exciting verbally and theatrically than I could have done by any other way.

Equally, I think that I was pretty intrusive into your territory. I do feel when I'm working on an adaptation that I have a right to do that, and I do jump on a writer and question lines much, much more than I would if it was original material.

I'm interested to know whether you think that was a good foundation stone to our relationship, and whether, when you have your adaptor/translator hat on, you are prepared to take more shit from the director?

RN: What's exciting about doing translation/adaptation is working with the director. I have no real ambition to sit and translate a play on my own. Whether I choose to do a translation/adaptation is based upon the work that's to be translated and the director who is to direct it. So a director is not intruding. It's a collaboration. Working together along similar lines on a new translation/adaptation in a production atmosphere, questioning lines and working dramaturgically as well, can be a very fruitful collaboration. It's a way of learning. I think that a director must tackle a classic in a way that's meaningful to himself and energize it for himself.

But the poor playwright who is being translated and adapted needs to be protected somehow. In the right situation, as was our case with *Jungle of Cities*, at different times we both protected Brecht and his writing from each other. It was very important for us, having worked together too long in an administrative way (as literary manager and artistic director) when neither one of us saw ourselves much as administrators. It wasn't until we could get on in a production together that we saw each other clearly.

But it can go other ways. When I agreed to do Beaumarchais's *The Marriage of Figaro* at the Guthrie [Theatre, Minneapolis] for André Serban, there were all kinds of problems in translating/adapting the play. I think it's the third act – the trial act – that doesn't make sense any more. It was written to make satirical points about specific people at a specific time. You have to restructure the play and so there's a lot of work to be done with the director. So I went to André's house in upstate New York.

André's method is difficult – he worked with me as he works with his designers, which is, basically, saying 'No' and often, 'No, that's stupid' over and over and over again to everything. He's looking to you to ignite him. 'Make it interesting to me' is almost the attitude. He's looking for that one little key – that tiny thing – and you have no idea what that will be and no idea about how to engender it, because it's not coming from anything of your own.

He's holding the artistic cards. Initially it was interesting, but as more and more questions came up, it became more and more obvious how little he understood the play to the point where, halfway through the first day, he admitted he had thought he had agreed to do the opera and not the play.

DJ: Did you believe him?

RN: He said he didn't even like the play. And after a day and a long night of this, I was going crazy. I think there are so many times you can be told that what you've just said is 'stupid' before you just want to run screaming into the night. Anyway, by the next day I'd figured I would just go ahead and do what I thought was right for the adaptation and if André didn't want it, then that was his problem. I'd had enough, and I wanted to go home. André said I could take the bus back to New York (and from there a plane to Minneapolis where I was then living) or, if I were in a hurry, there was a little airport near by where I could catch a plane to LaGuardia. Without a moment's hesitation, I said, 'To the airport'. I wanted that much to get out of there as quickly as possible. We drove to this 'airport' and it was a cow pasture with an old piece of cement down the middle. There were cows and there was a garage. André saw my face and again suggested that I could take the bus, but as the next bus didn't leave for a few hours, and whereas the plane was to leave within the half hour, I felt there was no decision. I couldn't stay another second talking with André about this play.

So I went into the garage/terminal, got my ticket and this tiny plane came in. I hate little planes, and this would be the smallest I'd ever flown in, but still I kept thinking, 'If I stay another ten minutes with this man I'm going to kill him.'

The person behind the counter in the garage said to the pilot, 'You got one more passenger.' The pilot walked by me, opened a closet and took out a seat, the extra seat they have for the last passenger, and he carried it to the plane and bolted it in. I got in and sat down. They closed the door and the pilot climbed over me to get to the controls and off we went.

There were about twelve people, I guess, in the plane, like eleven Japanese businessmen and me, and we had beautiful blue skies all the way to LaGuardia so by the time we were about to land, I was feeling fine, relieved to be away from André. Then I suddenly heard over the speaker, '747, 747.'

And there right in front of us – I could see through the front window – was a jumbo jet sitting on the runway. We were headed right for it when we suddenly banked up and turned, barely missing it. Or so it seemed to me.

DJ: It was smack in front of you?

RN: It was smack in front of us. We just went straight up and then circled and we were quickly allowed to land on another runway. Of course the Japanese businessmen slept through it all and only the pilot and I knew what had nearly happened and we were both completely wiped as we got off that plane.

DJ: What do you think God was trying to say to you?

RN: I don't know about God but I'd say that this is how I risked my life to get away from a director.

DJ: But you did the show.

RN: I was working as the dramaturg at the Guthrie, so it was very hard for me to pull myself from the show because in a sense I was one of the producers as well. I went to Liviu, who was the artistic director, and said I can't work with Serban but he can do whatever he wants to the script, and that was that.

When André was in his third or fourth week of rehearsal, I got a call from the stage manager, could I please go down to the rehearsal. There was André and his cast on a mat, all in a circle and all with bamboo poles. They had done three weeks of bamboo pole rhythm pounding and now they were ready to get to the script.

DJ: They were just about to start?

RN: André said, 'Sit, Richard, sit.' And I sat down on the mat and he said, 'Now, Richard, tell us again the plot of this play.' He didn't know the plot. Then he had the company divide up into groups and do their own mini productions of the play: 'Do something weird, do something strange with the play' is what he told them. Someone that day happened to have a skateboard and he used it in one of those 'productions' and when André saw this he said, 'Now I know,' and he put the entire production on wheels – skateboards, roller skates, shopping carts – wheels.

DJ: Yes, I remember.

RN: I was very lost because I'm a writer where images are powerful because of their meaning, not because of the attractiveness of the image itself. Here, with André, you're dealing with a series of images where no one is controlling the meaning. It wasn't until the show was done in New York that I came back into it and worked with his images.

DJ: Did you rewrite a fair bit of dialogue for New York?

RN: No. But I worked dramaturgically on the show a great deal.

DJ: Was he at that stage able to listen and use your ideas?

RN: Yes, to the other extreme. He was completely open and completely willing to do anything I wanted, because he had done the show, he was a little bored and he was looking for a way to get interested in it again. Do you remember all those cream-coloured costumes everyone wore in the first four acts, and then in the last act, everyone came out in black?

We were into the second week of previewing when André said to me at the end of one show, 'Now what do you think, Richard, if we do the first four acts in the black costumes and the last act in the white?' (*Laughter.*)

DJ: Do you think he really wanted an answer or do you think he was just trying you out?

RN: With André, I don't know. I could never know what his intention was or what he wanted. The only consistency that I could figure out with André was that he didn't want to be bored.

DJ: Well, that has to be a factor in the director's role if you continue after six weeks of rehearsal with a play. It's a question of what bores you. I think you get bored very easily if you haven't got a main thread of meaning. What you're talking about with André is the problem of being eclectic, surreal, non-logical. You can pluck amazing moments out of the air with that but it's very hard to construct a work that has a unified drive.

Do you think a lot of writers are seized about two days into a relationship with a director by a sense of panic and, 'I've gotta get out of here'?

RN: Um . . .

DJ: Or is it only certain central European directors of strong personality that have that effect on you?

RN: If you know you're working in the same field and you're trying to plough the same furrow, then you can always come back and say, 'We've ploughed this much field today or we haven't ploughed this much field, but we all know what we're doing.' If it's a matter of wild swings as to who is controlling the show, and you don't have a place to fit, then I would run away. If I can't help, I can either be in rehearsal and be destructive or I can get away, and I'll always choose to just walk away.

I think some playwrights are destructive for whatever reasons of their personality, but for those of us who aren't, I think it's a responsibility, a function, of the director to involve that writer. As you said, it's an incredible resource that a director can draw from and the director will end up doing a more useful job. Anyway, that was André, which, by the way, is not the only time that working with a director has brought me face to face with death.

DJ: When else?

RN: When I was in the early stages of working with Trevor Nunn on the screenplay based on Edith Wharton's *Ethan Frome*. Trevor had asked me to do this and we'd agreed that I would work very closely with him, as I had done, writing the book for *Chess*. That is, I'd write, say, five pages, show it to him, talk through it together, go back and rewrite while writing the next five or ten pages and so on.

In this way Trevor would never be wildly surprised by what I'd done and we'd have agreed together on the basic structure of the piece. It's a good way to work on a film, I think.

Anyway, we were a few weeks into the process – we'd worked for a few weeks in London and now Trevor was in New York, so we were working there. He'd gotten a room at a new hotel on Times Square, called the Embassy Suites Hotel. And when I came in for the weekend with a pile of new pages I decided it would be a good idea if I stayed there as well.

I was put on something like the forty-first or forty-second floor – the top floor. Trevor was about ten floors below. And as I'm a bit scared of heights and the windows in this hotel came down to one's ankle, this was not a great thrill, but if I kept the curtains drawn, it was fine.

So we worked all day Saturday and agreed to start again at ten the next morning. I got up at nine, got dressed and got into the elevator. The door closed and then suddenly there was a big bang, as if something had broken, and the elevator began to sway a bit, though it didn't move. I tried a few buttons – nothing.

It wasn't long before I realized I was stuck in a swaying elevator forty-something floors above New York. There was a speaker in the elevator, so help arrived soon, though all we could do was get the door open a crack, and at this point I could see that I was actually stuck between floors. More help was sent for – an iron bar was handed to me through the crack and I was told to bang at a lever which I couldn't reach.

An hour passed, and I requested that Trevor be told that I would not make our ten o'clock meeting. Soon after Trevor arrived and he was very concerned. He asked if there was anything I needed and I said I was hungry and he hurried away, only to return with a Danish pastry which he pushed through the crack. I thanked him for this and said I was sorry we'd lose the time working on the screenplay, at which point he said not to worry, and through the crack came a copy of the novel, *Ethan Frome*, a pad of blank paper and a pen.

I laughed, thinking this was a very funny joke, but I could see he wasn't trying to be funny. 'What else do you have to do?' is what I remember him saying. And so I took his pad and pen and book, and as every engineer for Otis Elevator within a hundred miles was trying to get me out, I did some work on our screenplay. I did of course get out – after a little over three hours.

Anyway, directors and death – as a playwright sometimes you wonder if there isn't a connection between the two.

*

But it's *my* play!
The playwright, in Bulgakov's Black Snow

We're talking of a great range of experiences here – different relationships: different divorces and different marriages. When a writer and director hold those first meetings to talk about the play, lots of different things can happen. I'll talk about the two with Roger Michell, both different: one difficult good, one difficult bad. With *Some Americans Abroad* I waited a number of months for a response from the RSC, who had commissioned it, for someone to direct it. It was on again, off again, it was going to be in this theatre then that theatre.

I hadn't talked to anyone about the play beforehand. It was a gamble for me to write; it's so subtextual. Even when I would read a scene without preparing myself for it, it would seem like there was nothing there. So at one point I knew I wanted to do some revisions and I just sat down and I rewrote the play without any feedback.

By this time Roger had agreed to do it and I said, 'I've got revisions,' and, before I'd ever met him, he called me up and said, 'You've made a big mistake. The revision is in almost every instance wrong.' And he said, 'I was very disappointed in reading it.' I remember him saying that.

DJ: This is tricky.

RN: It was tricky. I was stunned and saddened and I went back and, indeed, I knew he was right. I was forcing on the play a change that was really out of order. It was as if I was going to layer the play one more time so that it became clearer.

DJ: You were doing the work of the production ahead of the production.

RN: Yeah. I admired Roger for saying that and we got along very well and I used a few things from the new version, but basically went back to the old one.

With *Two Shakespearean Actors*, Roger came to see me in America. I had given him a couple of books he'd asked for about the Astor Place riot [a riot in New York in 1849, sparked by rivalry between the actors William Charles Macready and Edwin Forrest]. He said, 'Let me start by saying what I think was interesting about the riot and about Macready and Forrest. There's some interesting snippets that I came across in the reading that I want to pass on.'

I sat and I listened, and I listened, for about fifteen minutes and then I said, 'Why are you telling me this? I don't need to be told what is interesting in relationship to the historical situation. What I need to do is talk about the play.' In other words, I suppose I was saying I didn't need him to be creative about the source material, but rather to tell me what he thought about my play. And that of course was difficult.

What is amazing to me now is that here was someone who I'd just spent months and months with first in rehearsal with *Some Americans Abroad* in England and then again with *Some Americans* in New York; and there was that moment when I didn't know if I knew him.

DJ: I'm sure you feel that with me sometimes.

RN: I have. I have. But I also know now that he felt the same about me. Here was this writer whom he thought he knew, who was now telling him he didn't need a certain kind of input, and so forth. One minute closest friends, the next strangers. The intensity of this sort of collaboration, I suppose, can do that.

So, the first meetings – very cagey and very careful.

DJ: Were you very conscious of the fact that Roger was the first director who was younger than you? Did you feel you were either protected or bossed around by father figures before?

RN: No, no, no. I think that all the director relationships I've had – with maybe the exception of Liviu who has never directed one of my plays – have not been father figures but older brother figures. Father figures I can have a difficult time with. Until I was at least fifteen my older brother was the most important person in my life.

DJ: You're my best friend in America, yet I don't think I've had a moment's discussion with you about this older brother.

RN: He's three and a half years older; and when we were kids my family moved a great many times. My father was a business consultant and his job kept changing so we moved.

My brother was one of the few constants in my childhood, along with my parents, and he became for me more than a brother – a mentor, a best friend, a confidant, as well as a competitor who brought out the best in me. Today, we don't see each other nearly as much as I think we'd like to, for a variety of reasons. My point then, I suppose, is that given this formative relationship with my brother I am very very comfortable with other such relationships in my life, and no doubt seek them out. What I am not comfortable with is when such a relationship is turned into a father/son relationship, and I find myself 'being taught' or being told what I have to do. When this has happened, I am not at my best.

DJ: And this relates to your relationship with your father?

RN: It must. But the point to make here is that as a playwright I go into the relationship with a director potentially at a rather deep psychological level. And I would guess most playwrights do the same. As you hand over your hopes and ambitions to someone, you look for a someone who you will be comfortable with. I had a good strong experience with my brother, so I work with a lot of older directors. What makes a writer and director click can be something as basic as that.

DJ: In your published preface to *Principia* you write that you were obsessed by fathers and sons while writing it. That certainly didn't figure high with me as part of the energy thrust of the play.

RN: In the same month or two in 1983, my first child was born and my mother was diagnosed with terminal lung cancer. The effect of these two events on me was dizzying. I'd been living away from my parents for so long, I'd forgotten what it was or what it meant to be a son. My mother's imminent death made me think about being a son again; about growing up, about ideals being changed, if not shattered, about forgiving. And as I'd never been a father before, Zoe's birth made me think about who and what a father is; about finding something outside yourself that you care about more than yourself, about sacrifice, and – about forgiveness of anything and everything. Months later I wrote *Principia*; to me those are its themes.

DJ: But as it was your mother's death that haunted you and your kids are both girls, why isn't the obsession with mothers and daughters?

RN: Because the play isn't about my mother or my daughter (or my father for that matter), it is about me. About me becoming a father and about me becoming a son. To me that is what the play is about; but as it is out there now, for someone else it can be about something else.

THREE Stupid Questions: the Text

> Surely people understand that when one hands them a
> script, one expects them to read it within minutes, and
> comment on it both profoundly and favourably for
> weeks afterwards.
>
> *Simon Gray*

RN: We've talked about what attracts you to a play. Can you
talk about how finished you feel that a text needs to be before
you even get involved and then how finished it must be
before you proceed to the next step of rehearsals.

DJ: There is a very marked difference – though it's not
necessarily a difference between the media – between a script
written for the theatre and a script written for the cinema,
and my attitude or expectation is very different. I expect, or
would hope, that a theatre script being presented to me is the
author's last word as of that moment, given that we may find
things which do or do not work in rehearsal, things that need
expanding or excising then. While not being over-reverential
towards a play that excites me, I would always try to make it
work as written. I would regard the script as innocent until
proved guilty.

I feel very differently about a movie script, because with a
movie script it is much more difficult to strike a balance
between the writer's concept and the continual nudge towards
how the thing might be directed. In particular, American
film scripts tailor-made for the Los Angles market are to me
horrifically full of directorial comments, which I don't think
should be there. They are the sort of scripts that, however
good the dialogue, you want to throw into the corner of the

room, because they not only tell you at great length what every character is feeling at every moment between the line and on the line, but also they tell *you* what you are feeling about what the character's feeling. It's a totally manipulative presentation of the script. What I want is the events, the characters and what they say, then there's a mystery left in the story and I have a job to do. It's a sad but true fact that the stature of the writer in the theatre is tenfold greater than in the film world.

RN: Let's look at some examples. How did you work on a boulevard comedy like *The Return of A. J. Raffles*? Here's a case of a play that was written as an entertainment. At what point do you revise such a play, which might be in need of revision either because of your own reaction to reading it or because in rehearsals things were not working? With a comedy of that nature, needing an actor's specific and definite response, do you have any outward criteria, unlike a more serious play that carries the vision of an author who can then be the last arbiter of that vision?

DJ: Yes, that was a tricky one. Graham Greene was very fond of the play, but he would certainly have put it in the 'Entertainments' category of his work. It was a tribute to a fictional character that he was fond of and he had this humorous idea of an encounter between him and the Prince of Wales, which is the great scene in the play, though I think that the third act has some marvellous philosophical encounters in it. But it was something that he wrote in a light-hearted, amused way. I don't think he took its commercial possibilities that seriously. If it had been by a much younger, newer author, I might have said, 'I think that act one is a little slow in its exposition and I think the play across the board maybe isn't quite as funny as it might be. But I think it has a marvellous kind of nostalgic Edwardian atmosphere to it which I could get.' The play was not a blockbuster success and it was liked in a quiet way.

The interesting thing was that with this play he had re-turned to the theatre after a long gap, and it was to a theatre that he didn't recognize in terms of its working methods. He said to me after the first week of rehearsals, 'It's such fun not working with knights and dames all the time.' In the fifties, the heyday of his theatrical activity, his plays did have a major theatrical knight or dame in them and were part of the H. M. Tennent world. It was the old school of star theatre. He had been used to rehearsals being full of diplomatic games – 'Have we got the right costume to keep the leading lady happy?' – and the author being politely treated and taken out to lunch but not really being consulted at all. To find a group of actors tackling what was a lightweight work with zest and excitement was thrilling to him. He was very waspish about his past experiences in the theatre but he found it difficult to be immediately sharp about what he didn't like, so everything, apparently, was very pleasing to him. It was a good experience for me but my one huge regret is that if I hadn't been diverted by going back into television for a couple of years, and if *Raffles* had been marginally more of a success, I might have persuaded him to turn his attention back to the theatre. I think he was poised to come back but because he came from such a different theatrical tradition I didn't find the way to involve him more or send him away yearning to write more plays.

RN: Was that the case with David Mercer? You mentioned a blockage.

DJ: Yes, but actually the toughest thing with David – with any writer you admire and have been involved with – was when he wrote one play which I thought was a real disaster and he thought was marvellous. It's very difficult. It was about Henry IX, a homosexual King of England, and it all took place on the balcony of Buckingham Palace with irate crowds screaming below.

RN: But usually with David, when a script first came in, would you call him up? Would you meet him?

DJ: I'd usually call him and then have a meeting very shortly after that, and at the first meeting I usually just wanted to say, 'This is terrific and I can't wait to get started.' It was a celebration of the fact that the script had arrived. Then, and I think I started with David – it was easy to do with David, less easy maybe with Harold Pinter – I persisted in always having what I call 'my stupid question session'.

I will go through the script with a fine tooth-comb, and I will question the playwright if I have even the shadow of a doubt as to the tone of a line; is that an intended joke, is he deliberately lying or is he fantasizing, or doesn't he realize he's lying? You have to have courage as a director not to be afraid to appear stupid to your author. You've got to trust that the author isn't going to say, 'Does this man really not understand?'

Harold has been enormously patient and tolerant with me on that front. When I came to do the movie of *Betrayal*, this was the first time I really did this with him. I didn't see *Betrayal* in London but I did see it in New York. It was an honourable production, but I laughed three times, I think. When Sam Spiegel gave me the film script, I hadn't read the play. I read the film version on a train going down to the country in Somerset, and I just was laughing out loud time and time again.

I rang Harold and said, 'I think we've got to talk quite carefully because I love the script but I think it's hilarious and I believe you approved of what happened on Broadway. That was a different animal. That isn't the way I see the story.'

So we did sit down and I pushed him on this being funny, that being funny. A lot of it was funny, he said, but that was not the main point. I said, 'Even the scene where she gives him back the keys to the apartment and the affair finally disintegrates, when they're in that barren room that they haven't visited for three months, I think it's hilarious.' He said, 'Wait a minute. That's one of the bleakest scenes I've ever written.' I said, 'I know that, Harold, but the observation of the woman giving the man four chances to get back on the raft of the relationship and him just not realizing and missing the chances and being emotionally juvenile and stupid is very funny and satirical. It breaks your heart, but it's funny as well and I think that's important.' And Harold said, 'Now that I can understand.'

I'm sure it didn't date just from that discussion, but after my work on *Old Times* and the way I handled *Betrayal*, and the way *Betrayal* was received, particularly in America where it got an enormous comic reaction from movie audiences, Harold began to say that he'd always been a comedic writer. I don't think he would have said that at the time of *The Homecoming* or when the RSC did *Landscape* and *Silence*. There was then a perfectly proper seriousness of intention which was very Beckettian in the way he deliberately walked down some of the same road as Beckett did.

When I remember the original *Old Times*, I don't think it was very humorous. There was a sort of Henry Moore statuesqueness about the production which was a way of doing Harold that maybe was right for that time and it was a reflection of the way Peter Hall read those plays. I think my perception is rather different, is perhaps livelier and more kinetic and satirical.

I was very thrilled when Stanley Kauffman did a big piece on the film of *Betrayal* and said, 'What no one has realized is Harold Pinter is the Restoration dramatist of our day. He is putting modern society and the chic aspects of it in the dock and writing with an amazing social wit and humour about this.' It's not true of all Harold's work, but I think that it's very true of *Betrayal* and it's true of *Old Times* as well. It was interesting for Harold to find that the nature of the beast could change in different productions, that there isn't only the one way to do his work.

RN: In the American theatre there is a tradition – you could say almost a macho tradition – of writers rewriting up to and at the last minute. One rewrites in hotel rooms in out-of-town situations or, as it's now developed, for a series of organized workshops, staged readings and limited productions before rewriting again for a major production – all on the assumption that the play *needs* to be worked on and reworked. You don't find this in English theatres as much, do you?

DJ: No, although I think it's changing in England. It betrays a negative aspect of the theatre in America. If a show is not working on the road in America, there is a terrible tendency not to deal with the real problem – to feel that the answer is to fire an actor or to rewrite a scene when maybe the scene has not yet been solved. Actor and director may not yet have been able to put the key into the door to unlock that particular room. And the author may also not have found the right language to say to the director and the actor, 'I *know* that scene works.' Or the writer may be able to say that, but not tell you how it works.

I'm a great believer in battering away at the problem but that may be because I've done so much work on the classics where you can't ask the author to rewrite. You have the material and you have to make it work and that's part of your talent and your ingenuity as a director. I think the problem about respect for the text, and I now feel less purist about it, is that you can find in rehearsals that you need to ask for extra or for a cut. I rarely say, 'I think this scene is completely wrong.' I rarely want a rewrite as such.

The real problem of rewriting is who are you rewriting for? If the author is saying, 'I now see that scene on its feet. I don't think it works. Can I have another crack at it? I think I can do it more economically. I think I can do it more strikingly,' then I would never stand in the way of that. If other people are saying, 'It isn't really working,' and they go to the author and ask for a rewrite, then you have to be very careful as to who is asking for it. Is it the producers who want the scene to be more acceptable, is it an actor who wants the scene to present his character in a stronger light, is it the director who says, 'I can't make this exciting enough. I need a bit more juice there'?

There's a danger that you will write to formula or write to what people already know and will fit in with something they say they know will work with an audience. What I'm interested in is when you have no idea whether or not it's going to work for an audience, but you know it's exciting to you.

I think it's different in the more collaborative forms of theatre which you have much more experience of. If you are writing a musical, which is an amazing conglomeration of music, movement, dialogue and scenic effects, it is much more of a team creation than just putting a writer's vision on the stage. There, I think, the writer has to be – and I don't mean this is in a pejorative sense – much more of a carpenter and say, 'Yes, I can see you need another 4 × 3 inches of plywood to make that join work there.' That has its own excitement and needs its own skills.

But with an original piece of work, which is a statement coming out of the centre of a writer about how he or she feels about a group of people or a particular narrative or myth, I would reach for the rewrite pistol very reluctantly.

RN: 'Rewrite pistol' – that's a great phrase. Just to show how crazy a rewrite can be, let me tell you about the demands made on me when I did an adaptation of Dario Fo's *Accidental Death of an Anarchist*.

When we were in previews on Broadway, the producer Alex Cohen was very unhappy with two monologues that the Fool, played by Jonathan Pryce, had in the first act. He said, 'There are problems, I don't know what these are . . . the play has become static' and he was on my back to change them, and I couldn't understand what he wanted and of course he didn't know. Then Mike Nichols came to a performance. He had a good time, came backstage and said he liked the play. 'Is there anything I can do to help you?' he asked. I replied, 'Yes, call Alex and tell him that the monologues were sensational.' The next morning at rehearsal, Alex comes over and says, 'I want two more monologues in the second act.' (*Laughter*.) Nichols had done his job too well.

DJ: Did you write them?

RN: No, I didn't. So, it can be very dangerous when a writer agrees to make changes. It's a very tricky time because you have to hold on to why and for whom you're making changes. Once you start making changes for other people then you lose control of your own vision and then you don't know any more how to make the changes. You put yourself at the mercy of the people telling you what to do.

It's made worse by the situation that has arisen in the last fifteen years or so in the American theatre. People keep telling me they don't know how to read plays. I don't think hardly a major theatre in America will pick a new play until they have had a rehearsed reading of it or a workshop. Plays are chosen on the basis of readings that are rehearsed for four or five hours with whatever cast you can pick up. If you have, say, Jessica Tandy in your reading as an older character, then the play is much more interesting than if you have some young or inexperienced person playing the part. It's madness and it's crazy, but it's a way of saying, 'I must see as much of it up there before I can know what it is.'

DJ: I don't know how you can work as a director, or certainly as an artistic director, and not be able to read a play. If they really need those other props then they're in such a state of insecurity of judgement that they shouldn't be doing the job. It's like a conductor saying, 'I don't know if I want to conduct Peter Maxwell Davis's new piece until I hear an orchestra play it.' If you're a conductor, you should be able to look at the score and make a judgement, even if you say, 'Oh, that's difficult or I haven't heard anything quite like that before.' That's very exciting. You must, I

would have thought, be able to envisage at least two-thirds of
what the artistic experience of it could be. Such skill as there
is in our profession is supposed to make us able to understand
notation on the page, which is an indication of the artistic
experience we're going to see.

I'm appalled by this idea that artistic directors cannot
judge a play unless they hear it spoken aloud. I had a case
with a play that I was interested in doing and had no doubt
about its validity, a play called *Mrs Klein* by Nicholas Wright,
but the theatre in New York that was interested in doing it
was not sure. They had a reading for themselves while I was
working in Los Angeles and they were still not quite sure but
they felt more positive. They rang me one day and said,
'Could you possibly organize a reading for yourself in Los
Angeles.' I said, 'I don't need the reading.' And they said,
'You've got to hear it read aloud and then you'll see what
the problems are as well.' I said, 'I don't need to know
what the problems are. I can see what the problems are.
The positives far outweigh them. I don't need any persuading.
If you still need persuading, that's your problem. It's not
mine.'

Saw it last year with Uta Hagen

RN: That's exactly the position the playwright comes to.

DJ: It betrays a lack of nerve. There is a great deal of
conservative, take-no-risks attitude in people who are putting
on plays in America. George Devine at the Royal Court in
the fifties, with the immortal phrase that 'we have the right to
fail', set up a tradition in England where the attitude is more
one of 'let's see if what the author wanted will work before
we tell the author that it won't work because it doesn't fit
into the patterns that we recognize'.

There is, however, a certain rigour in American theatre,
which sometimes is lacking in England. There are one or two
English authors who say, 'You can't cut a word of what I've
written.' Not many, but some do. And there are other directors who say, 'Well, I know it's running three and a quarter

hours, but, you know, it's great stuff and we must present it in its entirety.'

We live in a world now, whether we like it or not, where the attention span for a serious play in the theatre is around two hours – certainly in America it's two hours. You can push it up to two hours thirty, but if you start to go beyond that then I think you are in danger of hubris.

For the first major original work that you and I worked on together, *Rip Van Winkle or The Works*, we only had a four-week rehearsal period and I was pleased that we hadn't cut it up front. As you remember, at the end of three weeks we were running four hours, and three days later were running three hours, and I would say forty-five minutes of that cutting came from *you* really knowing the architecture of the play so well and what you could afford to sacrifice and you going in with a kind of toughness and detachment to rip stuff out, which to me was a very, very rare quality. I hadn't worked at that stage with a British writer who could have done that, been quite so ruthless with his own work.

I think cutting, and the ability to cut with the author, is a straightforward if tough process. The one person I learned to do that a lot with in England was Jeremy Brooks. He did all the adaptations of Gorky that I directed. Gorky writes to an old-fashioned four-act formula. It's a nineteenth-century, much longer, dramatic experience. By the time one had fleshed out the life of those people, the running time tended to be three and a half hours. You've got to pull that back to under three hours.

Jeremy and I worked on a principle, which is one you and I worked on as well, that we would cut quite separately and then bring our scripts together and anything we both had cut would go and then we'd get some very interesting ideas from what he was suggesting and from what I was suggesting.

RN: What about in films?

DJ: With films I've worked on we have often started from scratch. I've built a script from nothing with Gavin Lambert and, with *84 Charing Cross Road*, Hugh Whitemore and I started – it wouldn't be fair to say from nothing – but when we started, we discovered that Anne Bancroft and Mel Brooks, the producer, not only were not interested in 'adapting' the stage version, but they'd never seen it. What Anne said is, 'Look, there is this book of letters by Helene Hanff – I want to be on the screen the person who wrote these letters. Can you make a film out of that?' That film was a shared partnership of building from scratch all the events we thought might grow into the world of *84 Charing Cross Road*.

RN: The difference between a film script and a play is that the film script is only a stepping stone to the event, which is the film, where the play itself lives on – or doesn't – in the culture beyond the individual production. It's unlikely that a screenplay as such will exist in the culture beyond the film, except for a handful of students or buffs. A play can have many productions but you can't imagine many films of a screenplay – of a storyline maybe but not of the same screenplay.

DJ: No one's going to put up the money for you to do five different versions of *Citizen Kane*, but Howard Hawks's version of *Citizen Kane* might have been very interesting. A theatre play can exist as a work of literature, even if it is never staged. There are some great plays that have sat on the shelf for a long time before they had a first production or sat there for many years before they got a second production. I still think, though, that a play is a stepping stone to the theatrical event which is the play in performance.

RN: And should be changed or rewritten for the needs of a particular production? I don't think I agree, David. To a certain extent, of course, one wishes to make the production work; but what if it's at the expense of the play? There is a possible conflict.

The difficulty for me as a playwright comes when something is not working out in rehearsal and I am convinced that the reason has nothing to do with my writing. At what point do I change my writing to fit a production? Or do I just leave it and say, 'This is the play I wrote. It's the best I could do'? Your attitude as a director would no doubt be, 'We must make this production the best production possible,' but you can see that there could be a conflict for the playwright.

DJ: I would hope, if you're talking of a specific case where, let's say, an actor is unable to realize a moment or a director has not really comprehended your intention, then you can eventually give the actor the ammunition that will enable him to tackle a part or enlighten the director so that he can handle the scene.

I remember very well there was a scene in *Between East and West* where the husband and the wife have separate memories of their arrival in the apartment and the changes were so subtle in your imagination that I as a director was clumsy. I was not apprehending what you were trying to do there. Once I apprehended it, I felt I could realize it. I'm not sure in retrospect that I shouldn't have said to you, 'Maybe there have to be broad strokes as well as these delicate strokes, just to help the audience a little.' To help me, too!

RN: Let me give you an example – this happened to me a number of times as a writer. When *Principia Scriptoriae* was in production in the United States, the first scene at the first preview was deemed by a number of people to be too long. It's a difficult scene. It begins in the middle of a conversation. If you know who the people are, as you learn in rehearsal, then it's quite funny at the beginning, but an audience doesn't know who they are so the scene is not funny. And so it seems a little confusing. I was told that I should consider cutting back the scene, making it two, three or four pages shorter.

DJ: In a major way.

RN: But I felt that it was not the script that was at fault, but something in the production. I couldn't exactly tell what. I was under tremendous pressure to cut yet I felt that I would be simply unravelling the scene. It was even suggested that I cut and we try it once, but I know that is a difficult road: how do you put it back in after you've cut it? So I did nothing and took the disappointment of the director and other people involved in the production and just wore that disappointment and carried on.

Six months later I was back in rehearsal with that play with you, in England. I made no changes in that first scene. We went through rehearsal. We got into our first preview and, again, I overheard one or two people saying the first scene was too long and confusing and I heard people say that to you. I went to the rehearsal the next day and instead of you suggesting to me that we should cut it or suggesting to the actors to speed it up, as also happened in America, you suggested the actors slow down. That way an audience would understand and feel confident with the scene. And, indeed, from then on that scene never seemed too long. To try to deal with the problems of the first production by cutting, I could have ended up unravelling my play, losing confidence in the structure and in how that scene was written to the point where I would have never learned in a whole other production that that scene was right.

I go back to a conversation I had once with a playwright we both knew, Max Frisch. I came to him with a problem concerning *Rip Van Winkle* and I said, 'I have the possibility of doing one very important production of the play or I could do another production where that theatre would allow other productions to happen simultaneously.' He said, 'Go with as many productions as you can, because a scene that people say is bad in one production often will end up working beautifully in another.'

It's a tricky situation for the stage writer as opposed to a screenwriter, but with a stage play, by necessity, your antennae are focused beyond the production at hand.

DJ: Yes, I understand that. What you're describing in the American production of *Principia* is that failure of nerve we talked about. It's to do with trying to do something radical in response to a real sense that a scene is not working, but it is bad diagnosis and therefore the wrong solution. I remember that scene very well in England and the feeling that I couldn't grasp why it wasn't quite working. As you say, when you get to know the scene well, it's very funny.

What Anton Lesser [RSC actor who has played leading parts in three of Richard Nelson's plays] was doing with those big speeches was terrific. I felt the basic truth of the situation was there, but I did know that an English audience would be fighting to follow the American accent at the beginning, which is why I suggested a slow down, and I thought that Anton was trying to be a little too bravura too soon and maybe if he went slower that would help. One thing you learn is that first scenes of any play are much tougher than they ought to be and if you could shuffle the pack and play them as if they were Scene 4, half the problems would go away.

I had exactly the same experience with the first scene of *Old Times* when I revived it. Mike Gambon, Nicola Pagett and I hammered away at the scene where the husband and wife sit and talk about strangers going to arrive. It's very light, it's very casual. It's about what they're going to have for supper and it continually baffled me because I felt it should be delivering something that I knew it wasn't, so we tended to get more and more ponderous with it. Then, when Harold Pinter played the part in America, he played it with a fastness and a lightness exactly like Noël Coward. Maybe the author could do that with his own stuff, with that absolute authority of lightness. It's a very difficult thing to achieve.

But I think you were right to stick your toes in. I don't think the director can say before rehearsal, 'I don't believe that scene works.' I can say to you that the play as a whole, or that scene, has got fat on it, it's too long, we've only got four weeks' rehearsal and let's not rehearse five hours of material. On the other hand, with *Rip Van Winkle*, which we knew was going to be too long, neither of us knew which were the bits that were going to be startlingly good in our production. We lived dangerously and flew by the seat of our pants. There is a certain responsibility to get the play manageable before you enter rehearsal, but not fine-tuned in terms of length.

The other thing you can feel that you have to explore is when something is missing, there is a void, a certain relationship breaks off before you want it to, or a character in Act I never reappears or their destiny is not resolved. I think it's fair to push for that if, as a director, you passionately wish something were more part of the story. But if the writer says, 'Great, but that's not the play,' then you have to say, 'OK, fine. Now I understand that.'

RN: What I'm constantly looking for – the hardest thing for me and the thing that I spend all of my early time with a director on – is simply, 'Does he get it? Does he understand the way this play is put together, how this play functions, its intentions?' If a scene like in *Principia* begins in the middle of a sentence, you want to spend rehearsal time on finding out what the first three lines before this might have been but only if it relates to discovering the structure of the whole scene. You don't want the director asking the actors to improvise lots of extra lines and say them as they make their entrance.

I'm trying to create a new form and this has happened to me more than once when I try to explain the structure I'm dealing with. It comes back to trying to articulate on the page something beyond the text, that's more than simply dialogue. It's the order to things and the way in which things function. If you write like I do as sparingly in terms of stage directions as you can, all of this matters immensely and must be dealt with. I can be wrong, but it must be confronted and not tossed away.

I can go back to the horrors of being a playwright. I can go back to the very first time there was a workshop production

of *Between East and West* and I came to the show halfway
through rehearsal. The text calls for a sparsely furnished one-
room apartment on the Upper East Side in New York. But
here was an unbelievably cluttered apartment and, even
though we were only in a 120-seat theatre, the kitchen was
structured so that half the audience couldn't see someone in
it. I looked and wondered how they were doing the scenes in
the kitchen and within five minutes the director was saying,
'Do you think you could change some lines?'

DJ: To bring the characters out of the kitchen?

RN: Yes.

DJ: The director was evading the problem.

RN: Exactly. He was not getting inside the play and seeing
what animal you have and trusting it. And that's the very
beginning of the courtship from the playwright's point of
view, when the director makes that jump of confidence and
then becomes the protector of the play in that regard.

DJ: Hopefully, what persuades the author early on is that you
do understand the play in a broad global way and there is a
real understanding of what the play is trying to do, which is
why it is crucial to me to have those 'dumb director' sessions
that I've had with you and with other writers where we go
through the play line by line. I do want to know the answers.
I want to be rock certain.

RN: I don't mean, David, confidence in the sense that, 'I
know it, I get it, I'll lead the charge.' I don't expect that
when a director sees the world of the play he'll get it all right
away, every moment of it; otherwise, why do the play? It's
more that a director should feel that the world of the play will
be a pleasurable world to be in and to explore. That he senses
this world and wants to be in it, as opposed to changing it. Once

the playwright sees that the director has reached such a point, which is a point of confidence *in the play*, then I think the playwright can begin to 'let go' a little, and let the director be the protector of the play, or at least of this essence of the play. It is at this point that the playwright and director begin sharing the play, and as they share, their objectives become entwined, and their relationship becomes a great deal closer or at least symbiotic.

*

Samuel Beckett knows what he wants. When we were doing *Krapp's Last Tape* I don't know how many different pairs of slippers he had me try. He wanted a certain sound from the slippers, and he wouldn't give up on it. Then one day before we opened, he asked me what size I wore. I told him, and he said he had some slippers upstairs and asked if I would mind trying them. So, he brought them down and we took them into rehearsal, and of course they fit, so I tested them out and he said, "That's it, that's what I want." Obviously, they were his slippers, and he'd had them for 20 years.

Rick Cluchey in interview

DJ: There's one thing I've been dying to ask you, and I don't know what I think about this. It's a semi-mystical question about creativity; we know a lot of poets believe that, with all their craftsmanship and shaping, in some way they become a vessel through which the poem expresses itself.

There are certain plays where it's almost impossible to analyse quite where they came from. They are not logical brick-like structures that could be written with the help of a guide to successful play writing. There is a daring jump of the imagination. Sometimes it's an entire play and I don't know, even if it's flawed, whether you can mess with that. I think very few playwrights would dare to say, 'This is a work of inspiration that arrived through me; therefore, I can't mess with it.'

But I do know that John Osborne would never revise and said, 'That's it. It's happened. It's on the page. I don't know how to change anything in it.' I do know that John Arden in his early work at the Royal Court, I think regretfully, was not asked to revise by George Devine, and that's only a tiny cavil against the marvellous things Devine did in trusting writers and doing their plays as written. With Pinter all I know is that when a script is delivered, he says, 'A new play has happened.'

We know that there's an enormous skill and conscious working that must have gone into the putting of that play on the page, but I do not know whether Harold revises a great deal and that's why the plays are so definitive or whether they're definitive because they came out of him like that. He did say to me about one speech – that extraordinary surreal speech of Jerry's in the final scene of *Betrayal*, where he makes his first ecstatic declaration of love for Emma – 'I don't know where that speech came from. It fell out of me faster than I could type.'

I think there is a fine balance between those incredible moments where the work just arrives and falls onto the page and the times when you hammer it out sentence by sentence and revise and rip it up.

RN: In writing, it truly is a voyage. What you end up with is not at all what you think you're going to end up with when you begin. Every play is like that and that's wonderful. That's the battle that you do at your desk and your self-worth is defined by how you handle what you begin with on that journey.

It's the part of being a writer that for me is probably the most meaningful, the most obsessive, the most addictive and that which gives me my self image.

The tool that I have as a playwright, the building block on which everything is based, is not the word or dialogue but people. This has been the biggest journey of my own career, that I realized it's not language but people. So, I start with people and I make those people richer and richer – as rich as I possibly can – and only a tiny bit of that ever gets into the language I use or into the play.

DJ: When you say you're making them richer and richer, do you mean in your imagination, as you commit them to action after action in the play?

RN: In part, yes. They grow that way and they also grow in terms of a feeling of what the people are. I purposely organize a scene to maximize their richness or their complexity. One product of beginning in the middle of conversations as I do is that you not only have to figure out what people have been saying but what they're saying in relation to what they might have been saying. You're allowing an audience to discover the people for themselves. You're actively engaging the audience and it's a wonderful way of getting them to see people's layers.

However, what's funny is that when I'm writing I don't have people in front of me, I only have words. So there's a very, very rich, sometimes exciting, sometimes incredibly frustrating, conflict or tension of two things colliding – the people you have in mind and the words that come out of you for them to speak.

DJ: Do the words come out of you or out of them sometimes?

RN: You don't know, but you have to be open. You have to be really open to allow things to be said in a way that you didn't realize they would be said. And then you have to be open to admit, 'That's a whole richer element of the character and not even necessarily the character that I had in mind. But I'm really fascinated that this person is saying it this way.' Now, what happens if that person's lying? Maybe we'll make him lie in this incident, and, oh, so he's the kind of person who lies.

Then slowly, through happenstance and luck and incredible amounts of revision, you start to build people who are slightly different from the people you began with. But you need to think through the repercussions of some of the things you might fall in love with, because, even though I never end up with the play I begin with, I always have an end in mind for the play I'm writing at that particular time. I always have an arc. So it's rich and exciting and dynamic. It requires that you spend as much time with your eyes closed, seeing what a new change means and running through the entire play with it, as you do physically writing.

In *Columbus*, when I was two-thirds or three-quarters of the way through, I realized that things were changed and I had to close my eyes and rewrite the entire play in my head with a new line running through, just upping the ante of certain elements of the play by twenty per cent and seeing how that would play.

And I wouldn't write it then. I'd say, 'Now I know I can do it. That's fine. I'll keep going.' Or maybe I wouldn't. There's a character Pulgar who was always intended to disappear from the play at the end of the second act and not go on the journey to America at all. But I realized as I began the third act that I wanted Pulgar there.

DJ: This is the Jewish merchant who becomes Columbus's secretary?

RN: Yes. And for two days I did nothing, not writing a word, but in my head plotted Pulgar back through the whole play and then I found I had to start the play differently. Pulgar just demanded to be on that journey. He demanded because of that point that you talked about of liking someone and wanting more of him and just seeing the natural growth of what happened.

DJ: That's extraordinary, because the dance of the relationship between him and Columbus is now the spine of your play.

RN: Exactly.

DJ: That's extraordinary, but reassuring, that such changes can happen. This, to a director, is a closed area. But let me ask you a banal question. How visual are these people to you?

Take the first scene of *Two Shakespearean Actors*, where the two rival theatre groups come into a bar at the end of a performance. Do you just think, 'Bar, tables' or do you see something much more concrete than that in your head?

RN: I see the dynamic. I feel the dynamic. It's not that you see where the tables are, but you know if it's wrong when you see it on stage. When I close my eyes and go through a play I don't go through lines. I go through, 'There's a group of people over there and then there's some noise, then a little more noise,' and I see everything in movement . . .

DJ: That's very filmic. That's like Eisenstein's story boards, which were not pedantic frame-by-frame story boards but impressions of key moments.

RN: That's it. I can go through the first act of *Columbus* in five minutes in my head. You learn what's the most important thing for you and it becomes interesting in terms of rehearsal with the director, because the way I now write is so much about finding out what's important in a scene.

Sometimes there's a whole page of throw-aways, people just doing the same thing, but many other things are going on that are more important than what is being said. If in a rehearsal there's an emphasis on what is being said in order to make it clear to an audience but the dynamic of the scene doesn't work, then I'm wondering, why are they paying so much attention to the words?

DJ: You must be the first playwright in history to say that.

RN: Sometimes I don't even care if people hear them. So this is what I've learned in this dynamic battle of people and words.

DJ: Do you always know what that secret dynamic is, particularly in some of your bleaker scenes, or do you sometimes know there is a truth about a scene that you don't quite understand yet and you don't know what the energy coil of the scene will be?

RN: That's dangerous when I don't quite have the handle on it. It's usually that I just haven't done it right. I think that the behaviour of a scene should be understandable in normal small behaviour. Where my scenes collapse or they're not written right is when I've had to serve, or I've tried to serve, a function of the play just to get some plot out or some theme out or to get the sense of an emotion out without anchoring the scene. I usually anchor it last.

I rewrote a scene in the third act of *Columbus* where Pulgar and Columbus are lost at sea and they're talking philosophically. Columbus is being thrown out of his cabin and has to move his stuff so I've got him going through Pulgar's books, throwing them on the floor, talking about ideas and making fun.

The same ideas and themes were in the earlier version but now the scene is grounded in an action – that of browsing through and throwing away books; and this action gives the scene its playability. Often, when I'm watching the director and actors having trouble with a scene, it's because it's not clear what grounds it – I just haven't anchored the scene right.

DJ: They may not have found the anchor.

RN: On the other hand, there's scenes like the little one in *Principia* on the porch, the penultimate scene of the play. It's a little wisp of a scene that is so underwritten in the best sense that when I thought it wasn't really anchored I found it dangerous to touch it.

DJ: I think it is a miraculous scene. It was extraordinary that you had the strength of mind to hold off from changing it. Some people might have described it as a pencil sketch for the scene that was going to be, but it actually has everything in it that you need. But if you play one line slightly out of key, if the actor is not emotionally ready for that line, the scene just slides sideways. No one's complaining about those kinds of difficulties, though.

RN: Going back to your question about when a playwright lets a director in. You talked about the process with David Mercer and about Harold Pinter, who would let the director in at the finished product. I'm learning that there's a certain point in the process where I need to let people in before I know I'm done.

DJ: Do you allow them into the park before the park is finally laid out?

RN: And to have an impact. When I first let other people read a draft I'm not presenting a finished product, and I know that I'm not. The danger in doing this is that a lot of people then think, 'That's the best he can do. We're going to have to push him on rewrites because we know we've got to get changes here.' That's a very silly response for me. What I look for, what I pray for, is that sense of, 'I see where you are. That's very exciting. Let me tell you my response.'

Then I know what has come to the surface, what has been communicated and what hasn't. If a director who is really getting the play comes back and says, 'I think this about this person,' then I can say, 'I didn't quite intend that,' and I can go and pitch something a little differently. I need to be at this level before I have what I consider to be a rehearsal script. It's a very conscious effort and one where I've now learned to need the relationship of the director.

DJ: But it has to be someone who truly understands what work in progress means. Otherwise panic sets in because people sense this is unfinished but they're not sure if you think it's unfinished.

RN: Exactly.

DJ: Many years ago *Monitor* did a big story on William Golding, long before he won the Nobel Prize. I think it was when *Pincher Martin* was coming out. He said four-fifths of his novel writing was brooding upon what the novel was going to be: 'I think about the novel until I have the entire shape of it in my head. I know completely what the journey of the novel is. Then all I have to do is write it.'

It's a little like Hitchcock who said that he found shooting movies very boring because he'd worked out every shot in his head. I find Hitchcock's remark almost obscene. Almost all the exciting things in my films happen spontaneously, in front of a camera. You plan for the exciting thing to happen but you never quite know what that thing is going to be.

Do you think Ibsen had a blueprint of where *A Doll's House* was going to go? Do you think he mapped out scenes for it and maybe only later, with plays like *When We Dead Awaken*, he just let things happen?

RN: The world is very, very rich and vibrant and fleshy and confused and ambiguous. Theatre should reflect that. That's the ambition I have and I think it's the ambition of a lot of writers. In theatre, if you aim to show life, you can't have pure forms. You can't have a complete right and a complete wrong when you are reflecting a mess. A wonderful mess, perhaps.

DJ: Just to hark back to this question of how far in advance you can plan the architecture of a piece. Thinking of your plays on a broad canvas – *Rip Van Winkle* at the beginning and *Columbus* most recently – I understand that you don't work out a synopsis of what scenes will be about, but do you find that bits from the middle of the story or towards the end leap up on you out of the night? Are you ever tempted to write out of sequence a scene which you think will arise in

Act III, say, although you know it could go somewhere else and it exists somewhere with darkness around it?

RN: I'm constantly moving forward and backward in the play.

DJ: Do you write those scenes or do you just log them and put them on the side?

RN: I log them as fragments, bits, notes, not as whole scenes, because the writing of scenes by and large has to do with the dynamic of that moment. The exceptions are those delicate scenes, like the one we talked about in *Principia* that seemed so fragile, and there's maybe only room for one of those in a play, at a special moment.

When you're doing a big play, the choices for every scene are not only what's going to take place, but who's in it and where does it happen. If you've got twenty or so characters, who's in it is a very big question because you have a lot of choices.

DJ: You might put all the wrong people in it if you try to write for Act III even before you've got there.

RN: While you're writing any scene, even at the right moment in the process, you can get three-quarters of the way through and believe you have it, when you think, 'If I could only bring in someone here. How can I justify bringing *that* person in? I can't bring him into this tavern, because there's no reason for him to be in a tavern. Where could I bring him in? Maybe on a dock, because he's a fisherman. Can I do this same scene on a dock? And now I'm on a dock, but then what are these two guys doing here? Now I realize I don't need one of them. I just need the other and maybe I can add a new character . . .' and so on. I put a play together that way, constantly going back and forth, changing within a scene, within an act, within the whole play.

Psychologically, emotionally, and in terms of my own

energy, I must keep a drive forward in the play. I can't get two-thirds of the way through and say, 'Now I've got to stop and go over it all again.' I keep going, because by that time, and as I'm getting older, the physical effort of writing a play is becoming greater. I don't sleep very well, as I wonder whether I can harness this thing.

The most thrilling time of the entire process – far more than the opening night or the first read-through or finishing the play to send it out or even getting the first reaction, which is very, very exciting – the most private and personal and important moment is when you're faced in your head with the reality that, 'Yes, it's going to work.' You may have half the play to write, but if the pieces have suddenly fallen into place, then you're happy. And the rest is doing it right.

DJ: That's extraordinary. You talk about the battle of writing a play, but equally you talk with a twinkle in your eye about this activity you go through in a solitary way in front of the desk every day. My experience of writing is minimal but I find the worst thing is the hours spent sitting, unable to start. Then, somehow, miraculously, at the last moment something begins to happen. Do you sit and just not know what's going to happen next, and the characters will not act or speak, or is that rare for you?

RN: It's not a problem I have. I've been blessed by lack of success. If I don't write, my family of four doesn't eat, and there's nothing else that gets you so quickly to the desk and wipes away all those questions of 'Am I doing it right?' or 'Is it important or worth it?' Finally, it must bring in an income to support a family. The battle is within this complicated world of making a living; how much can you just let yourself fly? I don't know what I'd do if I were a wealthy man and I didn't have to write plays.

DJ: So you never allow yourself to say, 'I'm not in the mood today'?

RN: I trust myself well enough to know that if I'm not in the mood then it's usually because I don't know what I'm doing. If I don't know what I'm doing, then it means that I don't know who the people are and therefore I can't write them and therefore I need to think more about who they are, and I need to goad myself in some way.

There are different ways in which to goad yourself. You could go for walks. Some writers will go for walks. But what I often do, and maybe this gives away too much of my writing and makes me into some kind of literary-bound person, but for the last five or six plays I've slowly begun to build a library for each play. I build up a series of books which reflect all elements of things in the people I'm writing about – senses of humour, historical periods, factual situations – and they're all goosing me. Sometimes the books relate to my personal life and that's what the spark is. But the goad is that, plus a series of notes, where I go back to try and find out what the hell I'm doing.

DJ: I understand that, because, in a much more minor key, I gather certain talismans when I'm working on a production. This came out of the RSC programmes, which I now think of as rather over-elaborate, where you put a whole set of quotations that didn't just fill in historical background but related to the thematic centre of the piece. Because of this, there were always certain poems that I carried around at the time.

Do you set yourself a target each day? Do you have a regular rhythm or pattern? Give me a typical day on *Columbus*.

RN: Unlike a novel or a large work of fiction or biography, a play doesn't have very many words. A play is, what, eighty pages? And if you write five pages of dialogue a day – what's five into eighty?

DJ: Sixteen. (*Laughter.*)

RN: So if you write five pages a day you should have a play every sixteen days. It's madness. The effort of play writing has so little to do with the physical act of writing. It's all in the thinking and the organizing. *Columbus* actually became the first play of mine that I wrote with music.

DJ: You mean playing music while you're writing?

RN: Yes. So, I listened to music, I looked at pictures and at lots and lots of books about Columbus and his time in order to find real things for particular scenes that would help. I needed to have real things that I could hang the weight of the play on.

DJ: It's a very tactile play.

RN: I have a couple of wonderful books that I would constantly look through, called *A History of Private Life*. They are bizarre French books where people have put together their views of what private life in the Middle Ages might have been like – what sex was probably like, or what a bed was like and what it was for, or what ordinary clothes were like. So I found ways of incorporating the real.

It was also a case of finding the places for the scenes. Once I could find the place I could do the scene. And because I knew the play was going to be very long, I knew that the way in which the play could break was if I didn't get a real good run at it. So I set myself a goal during the writing – and by no means do I write like this every day. I'd prepared for it for many months. But when I sat down to write *Columbus* I would attempt every day to write a scene and revise the scene from the day before.

DJ: In that order? You'd write the new one and then revise?

RN: More than likely I would revise and then write the new one.

DJ: So you have a complete new scene every day?

RN: Yeah.

DJ: That's quite intensive.

RN: But that was because the play is some forty episodes long and many are very short. When I got to the longer scenes, I slowed down, but also I knew which scenes would be coming and whether I needed longer periods of time, and I would actually schedule that. On my wall I had a schedule of when I thought I would finish the first draft of the play. And . . .

DJ: Were you accurate?

RN: I was early.

DJ: Oh. (*Laughter.*) Too easy.

RN: I was early by about three days, I think. There were a couple of times when I was stalled and depressed. You get into this rhythm and you think you're just pushing yourself into product. At a certain time I thought these days had produced nothing and everything started to untangle and came to a stop.

DJ: Hopefully you learn to shut up on those days. I still think the most extraordinary thing about a writer is that ability to stimulate yourself into creativity. Directors have an incredibly easy time. I can get up in the morning without an idea or an emotion in my body and walk into the rehearsal room and within five minutes there's going to be something dynamic which I have to respond to and the mechanism gets going again. What I find inconceivable is doing that for myself every day.

RN: Well, if you look at the other side, you have the difficulty of having to get yourself excited about other people's emotions and other people's ideas. In a rehearsal room, you've got to deal with more than just a rehearsal or just a playwright, whereas playwrights sit and watch people take their ideas and emotions seriously. When they're at their desks they are able to review and draw out their lives in ways that are rich and healthy. It's a very rich and healthy process, writing, by and large, because . . .

DJ: You can think about your individual life while you're writing – let's say *Columbus*?

RN: Oh, it is about me. I would include so much of me that, and I'm putting this simplistically, if I'm not well, there could easily develop an element in the play of someone not being well.

DJ: That I understand.

RN: I don't just mean that you put in the specifics of your life. That's often boring, at least to me, but your obsessions, your infatuations or your confusions are very rich.

If you say, 'The world to me looks so messy. You can't get a straight answer about anything and nothing seems to be honest or clear or direct.' And then by trying to reorganize the world and re-create it you can feel purged and cleaned and helped, and you can feel pretty good. (*Laughter.*) It's like a drug.

FOUR

Two Amazing White Breasts and a
Large Piece of Coal: Designing the Play

> After *Death of a Salesman* had made theatre history, it
> was published and the sentence that follows 'The
> Curtain rises' on the first printed page is 'Before us is
> the Salesman's home . . . an air of dream clings to the
> place, a dream rising out of reality'. However, the stage
> direction in the original manuscript that Art [Arthur
> Miller] gave me to read directly he'd finished it does
> not mention a home as a scenic element. It reads: 'A
> pinpoint travelling spot lights a small area on stage
> left. The Salesman is revealed. He takes out his keys
> and opens an invisible door.' It was a play waiting for
> a directorial solution.
>
> *Elia Kazan*

DJ: Shall we talk about design a little bit? I would never be
happy to go ahead with a design that I didn't feel had the
blessing and approval of the playwright. As part of the sessions that I do with the dramatist early on, one of the
things I will ask is how concrete are his or her ideas of the
physical environment. I love scripts that are not too precise.
With George Bernard Shaw, or indeed Eugene O'Neill, you
have a whole page description of a room down to what
books are on the shelves, and that is incredibly restricting.

RN: With O'Neill, especially with most of the early or middle
plays, he's trying to experiment in a theatrical world that was
so often very much lagging behind him. He was dealing with
people or situations that weren't used to serious theatrical
attention. In his desire to find his style on the page, as well as
in defining a tradition, along with Shaw, of the printed play
as a thing, his descriptions are very, very important to try to

explain his plays to people who wouldn't necessarily understand them.

DJ: I'm more interested not in how the writer wants it to look but what for the writer are the most important things in a scene. Then it's important that I have some solo time with the designer where, again, I don't push towards what it should be. We tend to talk ideas instead. Tim O'Brien is the designer I've worked with the most and we tend to talk concept. What is the play about? What is the feeling? What is the social placing of this group of people? Then I wait to be surprised. Tim is very open and I've found that our designs evolve a great deal. We go through two, maybe three models, although the basic bold first statement never alters much. If the design is *really* a *major* departure but I agree with it then I'll call in the writer.

Tim came up with a very striking design for *Old Times* but neither of us were sure whether Harold Pinter would like it so we involved him early on. If I'm convinced that I like the idea but it's not quite developed yet, I would rather take it to a further stage before the crucial moment of bringing in the author and seeing whether he or she approves or not. I rarely soften up the writer beforehand. If I think we're going out on a limb I'll say so and invite the writer to come and see.

Probably the boldest design I ever had for a living writer was Ralph Koltai's for Nicholas Wright's *The Custom of the Country*. I work very differently with Ralph than I do with Tim. We talk about the play and he will never tell me what he thinks his idea is going to be. Then he'll come up with something which I either buy into or not. It can't be messed with. For Nicholas's play, Ralph came up with these two amazing white breasts surrounded by a sea of sand, an extraordinary dream image which conjured up a lot of the Jungian undertow of the play. Nicholas, to his credit, was not appalled by it but thought it was rather fun.

RN: How awkward do you find it to have the playwright there?

DJ: To protect myself, the designer and the playwright, I would rather first see a model with just the designer. It's probably the biggest quantum leap forward after first reading the text and the first major meeting with the dramatist. The next thing is to talk with the designer, and you find out a lot about what you think about the play because you're having to explain to the designer. If the designer is going to shock and surprise, as I hope, then I'd rather look at that without the writer first of all.

RN: The relationship between a playwright and a designer is a very rich and important one and in the best of all worlds it is a relationship that one has both directly and through the director. I can learn a great deal from a designer, more so than even from actors. I can learn what I can do and what I can't do. I can learn ways of putting plays together. I actually wrote a play with a designer, an adaptation of *Journey to the Centre of the Earth*, with Ming Cho Lee. I wanted to see if we could create a new way of writing a play. I found that with the best designers, like him, Robin Wagner who designed *Chess*, Bob Crowley or Tim O'Brien, you have a free-flowing relationship back and forth.

I worked with Tim on *King*, a show in London that finally I was not credited with and did not wish to be credited with. Many of the few moments that were enjoyable were shared with Tim. I was writing the script with a model already built and a general design already approved. As I brought in new scenes I would ask Tim, 'Can you do this? Can this work?' and he would try, and he would have a new model for that scene within hours of my having written it. That's a wonderful dynamic, and in this case it was all overseen and orchestrated by the director, Graham Vick.

DJ: When we worked with Ed Pisoni on the television studio

production of *Sensibility and Sense* you had an entire second act taking place right next to a lake on a bit of rising ground. It's healthy that I can't remember who said what, but we came up with a solution which was to switch to a massive outer verandah in the Adirondacks. I think Ed, out of despair at trying to do a beach, moved us towards that, didn't he?

RN: I'm not sure how it came about, because I think I had in my notes at some point that we could do it on a verandah, and you maybe had it in your notes and I think Ed came up with the same thing. We all saw the problem. What I wanted on the stage was a sense of emptiness – the beach, the water and nothingness. Once you do it on television, however, you lose the sense of nothingness.

DJ: You've told me before that the top priority when you're writing now in a series of short, even staccato scenes, is to get from A to B to C to D almost with the speed of a film cut. You can never quite achieve it, but that's the ideal. Fluency becomes almost the most important thing.

It becomes a matter of taste whether you want to go abstract or towards the carefully selected, real object, which you and I have a very strong taste for. I'm thinking of that tap and sink in the prison scenes in *Principia*. It was an incredibly simple design by Bob Crowley and that was its greatness. But it was very important that that tap worked – that real water came out of that tap in the middle of the bare stage. I guess it was a very Brechtian approach to design. It was saying, these are the objects that make you feel you're in this place and that the characters, their lives, relate to.

We have no disagreement about the priorities: we should tell the story fast, there should be a concreteness about the chosen objects and there should be an overall aesthetic. You hit problems if an author wants more detail scene by scene than you can give and also wants to keep the play moving fast.

Some of Edward Bond's early work suffered a little, not so

much from the fact that it was over-designed, but that the Royal Court stage is a terribly difficult one in terms of wing space and flying space. There was a Calvinist purity about the way Bill Gaskill approached those shows which I admired a lot, but he refused to galvanize the scene changes so you had maybe two minutes of silence between scenes and then you'd continue. I thought that Bond's *Lear*, for instance, which I think is a quite magnificent play, might have taken off more in its first production if it had been much more moulded together, more fluid.

Would you like to talk to the designer without the director present? Do you find the director inhibits you?

RN: No, the opposite. I find when the director isn't there – sometimes a director has been out of town or can't be around – I find it too awkward because finally it's the director and the designer who must talk things through. I may give too much emphasis to something that has more meaning than I intended with a designer.

As a playwright, one's aware of one's authority in certain contexts. If a character needs to be reading a book and you haphazardly say, 'It could be an old volume of *Gulliver's Travels*,' whereas really it could be anything, you find later that the prop people have spent three weeks looking for that ancient edition of *Gulliver's Travels* when you didn't mean it like that. All because the playwright wants it.

Considering design is a very good way of talking about the play with the director and learning what the director thinks about it. You can convey your own feelings to the director about how the play needs to be presented through a discussion of design. A case in point is *Some Americans Abroad* in The Pit. When I was first shown the model for that set, with everything floating from the ceiling, I didn't know if it would work. As it happened, it became an extraordinary design.

However, when I saw the entire floor was covered by green cloth I said to Roger and the designer Alexandra Byrne that I thought it would be very hard to have real moments on such a cloth. I went back to your production of *Principia* and I said there was something about that wood floor in The Pit that was so real. I think Roger learned from that something about how I intended the play to be, that I hadn't pitched the play as a satire but rather as a Chekhovian drama.

DJ: It's curious but the boards of the stage, whatever that place is – whether it's a room or an old theatre from the nineteenth century – have a tactile reality that allows you to do all sorts of things. You can turn it into a boat or a seashore or whatever.

RN: That wooden floor in The Pit became an object of inspiration for *Two Shakespearean Actors*. I wrote the play so that at the end there was nothing on stage. And I wanted that nothing to be real because I wanted it to be a bare but real stage. I also wanted to play with the stage. In the *Macbeth* rehearsal scene in the play there's a trap door that the porter comes out of. I purposely wrote a scene in the second act in an attic with people entering up by stairs which should be the same trap. I was hoping to convey to a designer my playfulness in terms of the creation of the play.

The other design element in my work which has been both wonderful and frustrating is the title projections. Some people resist them, some don't and some think they're an admission of failure if you have to announce the time and place of a scene.

DJ: You're underselling those titles. They do many more jobs than that. They work as an ironic comment on reality and they layer reality as well.

RN: In *Some Americans Abroad*, all the titles were places. The play is about people being out of place. In *Two Shakespearean Actors* all the titles are times. It's a history play about time and compression of time. When we were preparing for the production in New York, I met with the designer and director and I saw the model which was great, but there was a question that had not been solved: what to do with the projections. I said that they must be designed in and then everyone saw how important the projections were to me and, I think, learned more about my intentions with the play.

DJ: I've never had any problems with that because I was lucky enough with *Principia* to direct the play where the function of those scene titles was most obvious. You had written a play whose title means 'The Principles of Writing' and the titles were the principles of writing before each scene.

RN: You even suggested there weren't enough of them and I wrote in the principles all the way through, which was absolutely right; they hold the play together.

DJ: What I love is that the titles are one of your main dramatic weapons, but you have never used them in the same way twice. They have a different function in each play, whether it's *Between East and West* or *Some Americans Abroad*, and therefore you have to find a different design solution each time.

With *Principia* there was also the boldness that Bob brought to the whole design. I don't think I would have had the nerve to do it with that bareness if it hadn't been that you, Bob and I had discussed it so closely. It was also a little bit of exigency. We didn't have much money, but that can often produce effective solutions.

RN: It was a set that I learned a great deal from, with just that door. I'd come from a production of the play in New York where it was treated much more naturalistically and had a three-wall set for the prison. In London I learned a lot about what I could do stylistically and dramaturgically. That set had an influence upon plays that I wrote years later.

DJ: You realized how little support you needed from the physical world if those details were absolutely right.

RN: Exactly. How that floor, that vase, that real place worked. How you could make that doorway, which was just a door, open up and there seemed to be a hallway down the way where you and the sound designer placed the sound so it was clearly coming from that source and was not just a noise behind a flat. In *Columbus*, every single scene is built around what you're hearing through a window or through a door, and that all came from *Principia*.

What about difficult situations with playwrights in designing? You've had one playwright – John Arden – rip down the set of his show during a performance, which expresses the extreme of all time. Any others? Or you can talk about that one if you wish?

DJ: I talked about the objection from John Arden and Margaretta D'Arcy to Tim O'Brien because of his family origin. I thought that what Tim came up with was very faithful to what Arden had written down that he wanted.

RN: And what John Arden drew in the published text. I've seen his drawings.

DJ: It was Margaretta who primarily objected to the design, though I'm not sure she could see what was there any more. There was an electric guitar in the combo for the music by Carl Davis, which I thought was an extraordinary score. I had asked them originally if they wanted pure folk. No, they answered, we want something which has a modern drive to it. The next thing I know is the electric guitar is wrong because it's a completely urban instrument. We should get rid of it. I think with that and the design it was much more to do with an overall dread that everything about the show had gone down the wrong road for them.

Mercer was always very happy with his designs. I did two

with Alan Tagg, who's beautifully efficient, and they were quite heavily naturalistic sets. I think in *Belcher's Luck* I didn't do it service. It wasn't Alan's fault because I asked for a very evocative, very romantic set of an old English crumbling estate. But as a result the critics and a number of the audience took the play as purely naturalistic, which it wasn't. If I did the play now I would find a way of making it clear that you were looking at a parable. Alan did a terrific set for *After Haggerty*, which, interestingly, used projections.

Then I worked with Hayden Griffin on *Duck Song*, which was a very surreal play. Hayden came up with a room which was just too big in the right way. It was cavernous, but also had areas downstage where you could confine the action.

RN: Do you think that as your own design sense has changed and the design sense of your designers has changed, that this has affected the plays you're interested in?

DJ: I think it's made me braver. I'm not daunted by a play that has thirty-seven scenes all in different locations.

I do think younger designers in England, having worked in opera as well as straight theatre, have a kind of panache and style which can be terrific. Sometimes it dominates or falls into the trap of telling the story of the play. The aesthetic approach can trap you into a design that is an art object and becomes the distinctive element of the production.

RN: It's a risk when you have a strong design and you choose to go all the way with it. When my play *Bal* was done in the Goodman in Chicago the designer designed a hill with lots and lots of gullies painted in a van Gogh broad stroke, bright colours and so forth. The play is written in about eighteen scenes, some of which are indoors, some of which are not. It was one of those cases of whether it finally fitted the play.

It's funny – you don't really know your play sometimes at the beginning of rehearsal, and I didn't at that stage of my career. What we found in rehearsal was a rather moving, quite simple play. But when we put it on a large, almost monumental set, the little twists that were very moving were completely lost. The final set was darkened into black and the show was performed on what looked then like a large piece of coal.

It was a gamble that failed, but much better to fail by trying something bold which may open doors for me onto how to write a new narrative or new ways of structuring and organizing a play, than to know where every scene is going and you just keep moving the furniture in and out. You can then end up with the parts being greater than the sum.

DJ: My visual sense is a little safe and conservative and I look to a designer to make me more daring than I might have been. But I believe just as the director is there to serve the play, so is the designer.

RN: When you're dealing with a new play especially, you are evolving. It's very dangerous if the designer's going to say, 'I've done my job. Now you can do yours.' With *Principia* Bob was constantly changing and cutting back and cutting back. There's a whole level of the design that he just threw out.

There's another case. I did *Between East and West* at Yale with John Madden, and at Yale you use student designers. John had seen the play as quite Pinteresque, in the way you described earlier Peter Hall's 'Henry Moore' approach to Pinter, where people are still much of the time. As we rehearsed, he realized that it was very much lighter, much more human, and when we got onto what was a big set, he watched a little bit of the tech and then stopped it. He talked to the designer but not to me and called off the tech for about five hours. He had five feet sawn off the middle of the set then, and shoved the remaining pieces together. The room became the right size for the play. It was a very physical way of seeing how your vision of what the play is changes in rehearsal.

FIVE

Eating Out Together:
Casting and Rehearsals

> On the first day of rehearsal of *House of Flowers*, its
> composer Harold Arlen arrived wearing a blue
> cornflower, with champagne and presents for us all. As
> he hugged and kissed his way around the cast, Truman
> Capote who had written the libretto whispered darkly to
> me 'It's love today. The lawyers'll be in tomorrow.'
>
> *Peter Brook*

DJ: Should we move on to casting and rehearsals? My credo
is that the writer has to be totally involved with the audition
process, well, certainly with the casting process. There are
some writers who maybe don't want to be that involved.

RN: One thing that makes a good director is that understanding of what you can do with, and what you can get out of, an
actor. As a playwright, I'm happy with the contractual situation that gives me casting approval because sometimes I can
say 'that's a mistake'. I don't do that often, because I don't
trust myself.

Being able to match the page to the person is part of the art
of directing, and I've been amazed many, many times. I think
that a playwright should by and large stay out of it, although
as I underwrite my plays so much, I'm starting to find it can
be helpful to visualize a particular actor in one or two of the
main roles. The television play we did, *End of a Sentence*
with Ed Herrmann, was written with Ed in mind. I was after
a quality that he had, a quality that was wonderful to see
explored.

DJ: Yes.

RN: That was an exception and there are times when it's a very good thing to work that way. We've had the incredible relationship with Anton Lesser who is an extraordinary actor for my work.

DJ: We weren't to know we shared that instinctive rhythmic understanding. With *Principia* he was to me just an exciting young actor who had the ability to cover the age span quite miraculously and who could do American totally convincingly. What I didn't know was that he would tune in to your music so well, which he just was onto immediately.

RN: It's the music that he's onto as opposed to the world of the play. With *Principia* and especially with *Some Americans Abroad*, he admits that he was well into rehearsal before he had the faintest idea of what the plays were about or who the character was that he was playing. He said the same with *Two Shakespearean Actors* but when he read *Columbus* he said he was worried because it was the first play of mine that he'd read that he thought he understood.

DJ: (*Laughter.*) Well, that figures. As with Anton, and I don't think I've applied this consciously, I won't cast someone if I know to within an inch what their performance will be like. You go for the actors that are exciting to be with in the rehearsal room and who, hopefully, will have some insight, which you can sometimes get with a completely unknown actor. That can be what the director brings into an audition, to see immediately beneath what the actor presents if there is this other frustrated caged person who wants to do something quite different.

Let me ask you: when you sit in auditions, which you have done with enormous patience, do you get very frustrated at your lack of direct contact with the actor because I monopolize the auditions? I *have* to find out in that fifteen minutes where the actor and I are coming from. It's an intense fifteen minutes of courtship and I find it quite difficult to accommo-

date other people who want to get to know the actor at the
same time.

RN: I've never wished to have any real contact with the
people being auditioned. I'm very happy to be a sort of
consultant who has approval as opposed to someone who's
making a decision.

DJ: Right.

RN: I'm happy to just stop a mistake rather than to make a
positive act. I consider that it's the director–actor relationship
being started and I sit there and watch. I have two difficulties,
however, with auditions. One is that it's so extraordinarily
painful to watch. In America, what being an actor means is
depressing. By and large they are good, talented, gifted people
and it's a painful world for them. The other difficulty is that
occasionally you find the director has not behaved well towards the actor. If they treat the actor like that, sooner or
later they're going to treat you that way. If they see it as their
show as opposed to putting something together, organizing,
creating in this organization, then they can just be very
impolite to people.

DJ: There are many more unpleasant aspects to the actor's
life in America than in England but basically it's the same.
    To me, the most important thing is: What's it like to talk to
this actor? Do I want to work with him or her? Sometimes
the reason for choosing one actor over another is not defin-
able. Sometimes it's to do with chemistries; will this actor
meld with that actor?
    But have you ever worked in a situation where casting
decisions were taken which you were unhappy with and you
thought were going to screw up the play and did screw up the
play?

RN: Not when I've been involved in casting. I have gone to

see a production that I haven't been involved with and I've thought that something could have been better here or there. But I've never had a director insist on casting someone against my wishes. At *that* point of the process of this relationship between a director and a playwright, you are desperate for trust. You want to trust the director so much that if you were to stand up to the director about an actor he felt so strongly about, then what would that mean for the whole show?

DJ: When I did *Belcher's Luck* I involved David Mercer very much in the casting and in the auditions. It was a revelation to me just how hungry to be part of that process a writer could be and how vulnerable he was if he felt that you were starting to cast without him. I remember David had not been quite sure about Sebastian Shaw and I really had to make a quick pitch for Sebastian, who had another offer. David, I think, as much because he felt that I'd moved without a final consultation, was quite edgy about that for a couple of weeks. As it turned out, Sebastian's performance was quite remarkable and David swore by him from then on. The only moment of tension between David and I was then, when he thought I had committed to a piece of casting without consulting right down to the wire with him. It was just a question of keeping in touch about something that was crucial, especially with a small cast play.

RN: I did have the peculiar situation of a theatre wanting to do *Principia* with the Norton Quinn character played by a woman. I said I would give it some thought but I came back and said, 'No.' There were reasons to do with what I said earlier about fathers and sons, to say nothing about the fact that the first scene of the second act takes place in the men's bathroom. So they cancelled the show.

DJ: Purely because of that?

RN: Yes. I asked the director, who was also the producer, 'Have you already cast a woman?' And he denied it.

DJ: They probably had.

Now we come to rehearsals. Have you been encouraged to come to rehearsals or encouraged to be there but then ignored?

RN: The worst period started in Los Angeles with my second professional production. I was encouraged not to come. I wasn't spoken to by the director. I was told that the director did not wish to intellectualize about the play. Since 'intellectualize' was used to mean 'talk', I found that very off-putting and confusing and distancing. I didn't understand what my function was.

DJ: Were there many times when the director was nervous about talking to you prior to rehearsal because he thought you would influence his approach too much? Did you ever feel there was an insecurity in the director at being taken over by the writer?

RN: That's exactly what it was.

DJ: I find it extraordinary, just on the basic human curiosity level, not to talk. It's a great frustration of working with the classics, that William Shakespeare is not there to be spoken to, but if the person who put the story together is there, I can't see how one doesn't want to sit down for a while and ask a lot of questions.

Maybe if the writer gets extremely categorical and impatient that you're asking questions and says, 'This reveals to me you don't understand my piece and the questions you're asking me about style show you're going to do it in an ostentatious or unhelpful way,' then I could see a director would get nervous and pull away. But it seems to me there's a depth of insecurity if you can't explore that territory to start with, to find out where the writer is coming from.

RN: I've had this sense of a director being afraid of me more than once, but never as great as that time in Los Angeles. Maybe I had all the secrets of the play and I was going somehow to kill the director's pleasure of discovery or I was going somehow to make the director redundant in the process.

DJ: Is it on a primitive level? They're afraid perhaps you will outshine them *vis-à-vis* the actors?

RN: That may be. But I've always made it very clear, or certainly as I've grown as a writer, that this need not be the case since I would gladly never speak to the actors. As you know with *Principia*, I was so quiet and sheepish in rehearsal that the actors were laying bets that I had not written the play and that I was actually a school teacher from the North of England putting on an American accent and it had been written by somebody else, because I seemed to have no opinion about this play. It's simply that the rehearsal room is the director's world, and that is that. You can't have a rehearsal room where that's not the case. That doesn't mean that there aren't times when I talk with the actors, but only with either the spoken or the obvious permission of the director.

DJ: In an ideal world, how much time do you want to spend at rehearsals? When you're in rehearsals, have you always been happy about what your function is?

RN: I think that it varies a lot. It certainly depends on whether it's a first or second or third production of a play. If it's the first production, then I like to be there nearly every day. There is a stretch of time when there's blocking and going over things that you don't need to be there for. From the moment you start not to give out positive energy, then you shouldn't be there. That's my rule.

I see one of the major functions of the playwright in

rehearsal as being cheerleader for the director. The more the playwright nods and smiles or laughs and is happy, then the less doubt there is in the minds of the actors. Removing doubt in actors leads to fruitful rehearsals.

DJ: That's an incredible definition, the eradicator of doubt!

RN: I'm more than willing to sell myself in that way, showing approval and making everyone feel comfortable. It prevents those moments if you've missed three weeks of rehearsal when everyone says, 'Is the writer going to like it?' and feelings of being very much the outsider and not knowing how to have a real input.

If you sit there day after day, you can have a relaxed input. You can find the right moments to make that input and you can put it in the right context – for example, 'Ninety-eight per cent is wonderful, but here's a little problem that I see arising.'

The contract for this relationship, since one is throwing all of one's weight behind the director, is that the director must not surprise. There should be no time in the rehearsal period where suddenly something that obviously goes against the play – ignores stage directions, for instance – is done that hasn't been discussed in advance with the playwright. It's very hard to be a cheerleader for something you're not confident in, and therefore you're put in an awkward position of either approving something that you don't approve of or not approving of it and perhaps stopping or criticizing it, and that's very unhealthy to the process. It's a very important rule but it doesn't mean that the director must only do what the playwright wants. It just means that the director must inform the playwright what he's about to do.

There have been times when I've gone into a rehearsal and found that there are three more actors in the scene than I wrote, even though they weren't being given lines. I wondered why they were there, and I had to wait half a day for a break to have that conversation.

DJ: To ask why, and to say it was not a good idea.

RN: If the director wants to say, 'I know it's not in the play. Give me half a day to try putting three people in,' then if I disagree, I wouldn't go to rehearsal until later and then I'd watch what he had done. I would give him room to do what he wanted.

DJ: There are some directors, you know, who are very, very nervous about having the author in rehearsal. I don't feel nervousness. I feel guilt about whether I am wasting this writer's important time. Are there better things he could be doing? As we know, a lot of rehearsal is slow and laborious.

The only time when I get restless is if I know I'm not working very well, if I know I'm not getting a scene. I think, 'the writer doesn't need to watch me wading in the mud here,' and that's when you sense the actors are beginning slightly to look sideways to say, 'Is this the way we should be doing it?' When the glances start flickering, then you can be in trouble.

I don't think I've ever surprised you in the sense of embarking on something not in the text. Sometimes I rattle you a little because I'll turn to you after three hours of not speaking to you and say, 'So what do you think, Richard?' It may be one fateful moment where your attention might have gone somewhere else or where you may have been pretty unhappy with the last hour but didn't want to come straight out and say it. I think that's putting you on the spot and should probably be avoided.

RN: It's truly up to the director. It's a putting on the spot but it's like in a court of law, a good lawyer never asks a question of a witness when they don't know the answer. If you're prepared for the playwright to answer that it is going in the wrong direction and these are the reasons why, then it's wonderful to have that openness and that willingness to change and not feel like you're going to lose control of a rehearsal. It has happened with us. Actors find that it can be inspiring, but it is completely the choice of the director to open that door, that Pandora's Box.

DJ: I remember you watched me struggling with that scene in the men's urinal in *Principia*. I knew it wasn't quite right and at the end of the day I could say to you, 'That's still not in gear yet. What do you think?' and you would come up with a couple of ideas. You never said, 'This is what's wrong.' It was more, 'If we do that and that and then that could be taken back into rehearsal and tried out.'

RN: That is a good case of being in rehearsal and learning. It's a scene that I don't think is terribly well written.

DJ: It's a very funny premiss, them being in the bathroom, and it was so startling that you felt, what do we need to do after that?

RN: I don't think it works terribly well . . .

DJ: I think you're being a little hard on yourself.

RN: Though it was while rehearsing that scene for the New York production that one of the most memorable rehearsal experiences I've ever had occurred. Lynn Meadow, the director, decided for whatever reason that she wanted to rehearse the scene in a real men's bathroom. So off we went down the hall to the john. One of the actors took his place at the urinal and as they ran the scene he pretended to pee. At one point, Lynn went to him, pushed him aside and stood at the urinal herself, slightly arching her back as she pretended to pee. She was showing him how he should do it!

*

I show 'em how to do it – and even then they don't know.

Henry James complaining in a letter about the actors in his play The Americans

RN: What a playwright can learn by sitting in rehearsal is the meaning of playable: what can work with actors and what can't. You watch their struggles and you watch what they catch and what they enjoy and you realize that you can write very deftly and give them a lot of colour. You know how to play to them, which is what a writer sometimes does – plays to the actor so they're happy in what they're doing.

There's no way in which I think one can develop as a playwright without spending a great deal of time watching actors. A lot of playwrights have been actors and I think that the uniqueness, the positive thing, that those playwrights have is the understanding of what's playable. For someone who's not an actor, like myself, it's something that I've had to learn and I've learned it in the rehearsal room.

DJ: What is great for the director is the sense of a real strong bonding in front of the cast between yourself and the writer, that you are a team and that you're with the actors in that whole creative act that's going to be the play. It is great at the end of the day to be able – not necessarily as a regular or ritual thing – to post-mortem, to be able to say, 'Why do you think that isn't quite working? Didn't you think that was really major what we did with that scene today?'

RN: Or simply to say, if you feel something good is happening but the director may be doubting it, 'I think you're on target. Keep going because everything seems right to me.'

DJ: The biggest thing that I learned as a director was with the cast of *The Silver Tassie* when I was able to sit down and say, 'I've tried everything in this first scene. It doesn't work. I don't know why. I don't know what to do. Let's talk about it.' That was very important for me. It's very good to be able to be doubtful. We all have that little dark demon inside that is telling you, 'This is shit.'

The three authors I have worked with who have been non-stop in rehearsal are yourself, Nicky Wright and John Arden.

Nicky, like yourself, is incredibly discreet and quiet, but he does have a lot of fun. He actually enjoys the rehearsal, so you do get this positive feeling from that. Being a director himself he loves watching the power battles. He doesn't miss a trick.

Working with John Arden was interesting because John was very assertive of his author's rights and would very frequently comment. I had decided early on to make it an open forum. So whenever John wanted to say something, I gave him the floor and he said it. The actors for about a week were really baffled by this and they said, 'Please, can we stop these comments.' I said, 'Just listen, because what he's saying is very cogent.' It was mainly to do with the emotional thrust of a scene or emphasis. He would say, 'What I see this scene as being about is . . .' and he was always marvellous.

The difficulty came when he went further and said to the actors, 'What you should do is . . .' and he was always wrong. He always talked in external behaviour terms, never coming from the inside. I said to him, 'You've just got to hold off on those bits.' It was a continual challenge on the rehearsal floor and a bit exhausting. But I don't regret a minute of the time spent in that way, and the actors eventually found it invigorating. I was sorry to be deprived of his detailed comments once we got into the preview period and he was boycotting the production.

With David Mercer and Graham Greene it was a very different matter. They were bored by the minutiae of blocking and of thrashing problems out with actors. The pattern I had with David was established with the first play, *The Governor's Lady*. The title part was played by Patience Collier, an excellent character actress, but a very tough, rigorous lady. She would never stop asking questions. She always wanted the props there from the first rehearsal and she dominated the rehearsal room in a quite extraordinary way, but in a way which was always to do with the part in the play. It was a massive ego, but not to do with, 'Is this good for Patience Collier?' She was a great believer in 'the author knows best'.

I was a relatively young director. She and I got along tremendously well, but whenever David was at rehearsal, she would pounce on him and if he was there at lunch time he could not go out to lunch. She'd say, 'I'm having my sandwiches . . . I need to talk to you. You'll sit here.' She'd sit David down and pump him about the play all through lunch break. After about three days, David says to me, 'I don't think I can take this any more. Can I just leave you alone to get on with it?'

He found the nitty-gritty and small-change of rehearsal pretty boring, as I think a lot of playwrights do, but liked to come to the beginning. So, the pattern that I established with David after that was that he would come to the first read-through, and I would always like him to say a few words. He was usually very diffident about saying anything very much. He then didn't much want to come back – maybe once or twice a week for an hour or so – until run-throughs, which he attended religiously. He would see enormous jumps and changes. He was like a new eye. He was always very, very good on where the pitch of the character was. If something wasn't working out or I didn't understand something, he was always on the end of the phone.

Greene, in a way, was the most daunting person to have in the rehearsal room, but he was like a boy in a sweet shop. He was excited by actors, particularly the female ones. He was a kind of rehearsal junkie once he discovered something that excited him.

RN: The relationship between the director and the playwright during rehearsal is one of the most intense and one of the most fruitful there is in the theatre. Maybe it's an art. It is a time of mutual need. The playwright is watching someone take your play and interpret it for you. So there's a sense of an almost unbelievably generous act in that regard.

On the other hand, there are gains for the director from that relationship. It's an extraordinary bonding time. You go through ups and downs and through so much. Working on the show with Trevor Nunn, there was a whole year when I had more dinners with him than I did with my wife.

DJ: On *Chess*?

RN: On *Chess*. Same with Liviu.

DJ: Are you saying we don't eat out enough?

RN: Oh, we did. We have – especially in bars. It's the need at that point. The need of that involvement. If you've said, 'I'm going to filter everything through that person,' then that's an incredible amount you're focusing on the director. You're looking for approval and understanding and respect and care. When that doesn't happen, and obviously there are times when you find you don't want to go out with the director, it makes the entire production pale and boring and not right, not of life.

DJ: I understand that.

RN: It's almost that the relationship between the director and the playwright is the most life-giving for the playwright. You're dealing with people who are very smart and articulate and manipulative. Your challenge is great in dealing with that very live force.

DJ: I sometimes think I've talked less than honestly about how 'selflessly' I was trying to serve the play and the author, so it's very nice to hear you say that watching the director is your conduit for the play. At the end of the road, though, I know in my heart that what drives you in rehearsal as a director is that you do the play for you, the director. You start to tell the story in the way that has the most personal impact on you, that excites and moves you the most to watch.

Your biggest safety net is your own boredom threshold. It's OK as long as the scenes in rehearsal remain interesting, as long as you want to go into the theatre to see the show, to see that scene because something is being created which is slightly different every night.

Now I can imagine that in a very subtle, maybe not perceptible way, the playwright's 'child' moves over and becomes the director's 'child'. Do you ever feel that the director has become over-proprietorial and transformed your play into his vision?

RN: There are times when that happens in both a positive and a negative way. If the director's vision is broad enough, if he's good enough and if he understands the play well enough, then his vision can encompass your vision. The two are not in conflict but compatible and symbiotic. On the other hand, where a director's vision – or smallness of vision – restricts your play and makes it seem more theirs than yours, then that's unfortunate and it's not a relationship to evolve or one that will evolve in a healthy way.

There is a funny rhythm that happens in rehearsal in the relationship between the playwright and the director. It is a process of symbiosis and of separateness. You can't say that it happens every time or in the same way, but it is to do with the very rich needs of both of you. Early on the playwright needs the conduit and the director needs the support system. Then something happens after a week or so, depending on how long the rehearsal, where the director starts to see the light at the end of the tunnel and his need for the playwright is not as great. Then in the tech [technical rehearsal] the playwright is useless to the director, who doesn't really want him around at all. But what happens next immediately changes this. Once the play is in front of an audience, it is the director almost invariably who I found seeks out the playwright to bond again, because now the director has lost control over the product.

It's an emotional relationship the two have that no other two people have. They've gone through a process together and they're now exposing their work together. The director's work is very much dependent on the play and the play on the director's work. The two creative acts are completely merged on that stage and neither playwright nor director is really in control any more because now the actors are performing the show.

DJ: Yes, I think that is what does happen. But I'm very aware that there is a period in rehearsal when, if you're absolutely honest, you don't care what the playwright thinks. It's not that you don't want the author there. It's just that you know where you're going. I don't know where that click happens.

I had an old mentor when I first worked in television – an extraordinary guy called Huw Weldon, who was the editor of *Monitor* that I worked on. He would look at rough cuts, he would shake his head and he'd say, 'The trouble is you didn't fuck the story. You've got to fuck the story every time.' It was like saying, 'You are playing at this. It's perfectly OK. It's orderly but it's boring. Why didn't you go out and put yourself, everything you feel and think and know, totally behind what you're doing?'

I always felt that nothing I did really measured up to his standards when I was in documentary film-making. It was both very challenging and slightly daunting. When he came to see *The Lower Depths*, he said, 'Now you are fucking the story.' It wasn't a phrase he used all the time but he came out with it and it was very important to me to hear it again.

That moment in rehearsal becomes a very driving almost selfish time and you do know you appear to be unappreciative of the playwright's presence.

RN: There are also times when the director's on a roll in that way but the director makes mistakes. It's a very difficult time then and there's real tension when a director's on a roll wrestling it in a certain way and the playwright thinks he's wrestling it wrong. If the relationship isn't strong, that's when it cracks and the director gets frustrated and starts to think, 'I'm directing a play that doesn't work.'

DJ: I always feel it's my fault. This must work somehow, somewhere. (*Long pause.*)

RN: The building blocks of the relationship go back to those first meetings, to a trust built up through those discussions of the play and the casting of the play and the design, and the playwright feeling confident that the director does understand the play. If the playwright feels the director is going off in a different direction and yet he can bring this up even though the director may not agree, at least the playwright can say, 'The director does understand the play, so let's see. Give him a chance.'

If, however, you don't have the building blocks, if the playwright's been kept at arm's length from the beginning or the relationship is distant, then you don't have trust at those points in the process and you have chaos or you have hell and you have two people battling out their drive.

DJ: There is a period – it can be towards the end of the rehearsal but it's usually through the technicals and into the first previews – when I'm over-reactive to criticism. I know I've been very short with you when you've said to me, 'That isn't working,' and nearly always the righter you are the shorter I am. I probably have to sleep on it and then realize what it is you're saying and use it.

RN: Just as a director needs to pick the right moment to talk to the playwright about his play, the playwright has to learn to find the right moment to talk to the director.

DJ: And that's great when it happens. But it's also to do with the fact that the director is dealing with this other very demanding, very needing-to-express-itself creature, the actor, and a lot of actors together at the same time. There's the whole question of the actor and the book, particularly with scripts like yours and Harold Pinter's which are so carefully notated in terms of spacing, timing, pauses – which are not musical notations but indications of an event happening between the lines. If a director has worked with an actor before, he usually knows when it matters if the actor gets off the book even though he's not word perfect. People working with me for the first time will think I am letting a lot of stuff through the gate, but I'll get onto it.

The person who used to get most edgy about that was Jeremy Brooks who was like a hawk in protecting the sacredness of the translation we had finally arrived at. An actor puts his book down for the first time and I would have to say, 'I know he's got that speech wrong. Give him a week and then we'll get him.'

RN: It's a process of learning. In rehearsal of the first production of a play it's very important how the playwright reacts when the actors begin to put their books down and they begin to mis-speak. It's a real moment at which the rest of the production is going to be decided. I've learned to be incredibly supportive and say, 'Don't worry about the lines. Take your time. I'm amazed how well you know the speeches now.'

DJ: They know you're not sitting there like a censor.

RN: The bad side – and this is where one needs the director and the trust in the director – is where actors paraphrase, understandably so, and get into a scene but the scene starts not to work because their paraphrase is not as precise as your script. If they simply said the line as it had been written, the scene would work much better. I've had many cases where there's been no one vigilant on the book. No director telling a stage manager to follow the text. I've been in situations where people are asking, 'How do we make this work?' and then someone opens up the book and realizes there's a stage direction there that tells them how to make it work. If you give up protecting your script in terms of accuracy at certain points, then someone further down the line must protect it for you.

DJ: That's very interesting. You're right about stage directions. Three or four times I really blocked on Gorky, and he doesn't have a lot of stage directions, but every time I've gone back, and there's been a stage direction I'd misunderstood or there was a character leaving or coming that I wasn't aware of that makes the thing work.

I learned from being married to an actress about the process of making a speech entirely your own. You could be word perfect at home, you go into rehearsal and half has gone out the window because of pressure and thinking of other things and being nervous.

It's a painful time for the dramatist and a frustrating time for the director, because you may as well shut up for three days and just let the actors come through that particular sound barrier.

RN: I've found that Roger [Michell] has used what he called a 'beat' monitor for *Some Americans Abroad* and *Two Shakespearean Actors*.

DJ: Does he really have a metronome?

RN: No, no. What he does is, late in rehearsal, as the actors have learned their lines, he has someone circle the 'beats' being missed, and then comes back after to pursue it. I think that is very healthy for certain things. It explains the rhythm of the play, because what happens in a play is expressed in the learning of the lines.

Say you've written five lines in a row and they're for five people around a dinner table who are just having a conversation – quick, overlapping even. If the actors don't have their lines, suddenly you find people, even directors, willing to put business into those lines. No one's really looking at the end result, and you realize that you have a scene full of lots of things where everything is too important.

You have to keep in mind the music of the piece, the big long chunks of dialogue that flow over each other, and those that don't. It's a dangerous time when things can get blown away.

DJ: You mentioned a 'beat' monitor. Once in my career, when I was working in Stratford, Ontario for the first time, on *Twelfth Night*, everybody was taking a half-second to a second pause before they started their next speech. They all denied doing it. So I got a little . . .

RN: Metronome?

DJ: No, I got a bell, and every time there was a pause, I rang it, and I could usually get three rings in between speeches. The actors were fit to kill me by the end of the day, and I only did it for one day.

RN: With one play we had a run-through the afternoon of the first dress. Same place, same actors, but the performance that night was fifteen minutes longer. How do you add fifteen minutes to a play?

DJ: Easy, easy, particularly if you've got an audience out there, because you're trying to explore certain things. It's the 'pause disease'.

RN: The question is: does the director understand my music, or is he now in love with his actors and his business and his moments? It's a crucial test to ask, 'Do you hear the music of the scene?' And then, just as importantly, 'Do you hear the music of the whole play?' And that's a very hard one.

DJ: You may hear the music but is it important enough for you to shed blood to achieve it?

RN: The playwright has a real fear of being misunderstood – what those 'beats' or what those pauses or what those little directions mean. I got a query from a German director who wanted to know if every 'beat' meant there was a beat of a drum, which would have made the play very bizarre.

DJ: (*Laughter.*) This production I want to see. (*Pause.*) Do you ever feel ambushed by actors in rehearsal? Do you ever feel they are trying to get information from you that you're leery of giving or do you actually have a pretty good relationship with actors?

RN: I think you're always ambushed. There's always one or two or three people who want to talk to you privately, and you can't avoid it, because you go to the bathroom and someone's there while you're peeing, someone wants to talk about your play and their role. Sometimes it's just generous enthusiasm for being in the play, especially if it's a smaller role. And there are people who want just to talk about the play and that's really charming and wonderful. I'm very happy to talk in general terms.

When it's about a particular role I say, 'That's interesting. We should talk to the director.' I'm not a director, I'm not the best person to articulate certain things to manoeuvre an actor into doing the play as one wishes it to be done. That's not my ability or talent. The fear is that if I were to say something to an actor it could be misconstrued. We'd go into rehearsal and when we got to that scene and the director was explaining it one way the actor says, 'Oh, well Richard thinks it's this.' That immediately undercuts the director. Information is being passed that he doesn't understand or control and now the contract is broken because the director is surprised.

There are exceptions to this, because you build long-standing histories with people. I'll spend social time with Anton Lesser, say, and you can't not discuss the play he's in. The late Seth Allen played in a great number of my plays and we developed an important connection outside of rehearsal too. He wanted to know if he was going to be good, to make the play better. He didn't try to split the writer and the director, which can happen if the building blocks aren't there. If the playwright just drops in now and again or doesn't show much enthusiasm, then the actor who is dissatisfied with a director can unload the problem onto the playwright. This can't happen if the playwright has been there all along, appreciative and supportive. So, it's rare that I'll talk to actors about their roles.

I'm very happy to sit with a director and an actor who wants to talk about the play and I've had a number of cases where both the director and the actor have disagreed with me and that's OK.

The best situation to get to is if you can become not the 'answer' person, but a person who other people are willing to listen to for opinions and not facts.

DJ: The clearest image of closeness of actors, director and author I can remember is the revival of *Endgame* with Patrick Magee and Jack MacGowran which they did in 1964 just after I joined the RSC. Beckett came over and Donald McWhinnie directed it.

At the end of each day they would take chairs – I think quite unconsciously – and they would pull them into a cruciform shape, with their knees touching and their heads bent over together. You could not hear three yards away what was being said. It was like a confessional. It was tough on the two who were playing the characters in the dustbins because they weren't part of the inner club – or maybe they would have spoiled the shape of the cross – so they would say, 'Bye, see you tomorrow,' and the other four would go into the cross together.

SIX A Lot of Fear in the Air: Producers, Previews and Critics

'You and Mr Whitemore think you have created this marvellous Italian Renaissance roof of beautiful mosaic tiles. I do not deny every one of these tiles may be a fucking masterpiece. The fact is there are too many tiles and the roof is too big. And I'm not going to be the barbarian who goes in and starts ripping the tiles off. You and Mr Whitemore had better get rid of some of these tiles or this movie is not going to get made!'

Producer Mel Brooks discussing the screenplay of 84 Charing Cross Road *with David Jones*

RN: We know there are plenty of things that can upset the harmony of rehearsals in their later stages. No director, unless he runs his own theatre, can truly protect the play from others, be they producers, or people brought in from outside, or whatever . . . Perhaps if he has a solid contract . . .

DJ: Or has enough clout within that particular theatre to say, 'Fuck off,' if someone tries to interfere.

RN: Or it can even come down to tradition. You maybe haven't had enough experience in the United States to see just how often a director is second guessed and how, when you sit in the run-through of a play, there are twenty people all watching your show ready to interfere. One of the wonderful things, among many, about the RSC is that once a director is chosen, it seems to be his show. (*Laughter.*) . . . You laugh. This is what I have seen by and large.

DJ: In the vintage years of the sixties and seventies there was a lot of either official or unofficial double guessing, and your fellow directors did come to previews. They very rarely had the power to say, 'Change it.' If they were Peter Hall or Trevor Nunn they could, yet, it's very interesting, because one had to resist that sometimes.

The breakthrough production that launched Trevor as a director in the British theatre was *The Revenger's Tragedy*, where he and Christopher Morley, the designer, had decided to do all the costumes in black and silver. Peter Hall and John Barton came to an early preview and they were appalled. They were used to a kind of 'colour coding' of opposing families and, aesthetically, they thought it was extremely boring to work in a single palette. They did everything in their power to get those costumes changed, and they were even subversive with the company, suggesting that their acting performances were being screwed up by these costumes and by this production concept.

Thank God the company and Christopher and Trevor were unified enough to oppose this. I suppose the aesthetic pressure is easier to handle than the panic economic pressure of 'is this going to be a success or a failure?', which is a different ball game. 'If we open *The Revenger's Tragedy* in silver and black we're going to lose a lot of money, or we're going to get a bad review in the *New York Times*.' This wasn't said. It was just, 'We don't do things this way in the Royal Shakespeare Company,' which, nevertheless, is its own kind of pressure.

RN: One commercial show I did, after the read-through on the first day of rehearsal, the producer said to the lead actor, 'Any time you want the director fired, let me know' – the first day of rehearsal! I heard him say this! On the one hand, though, a producer can be the gel which holds the writer and director together and gives you the security to be a unit. When I talked about Liviu and the difficulties of doing the translations for *Don Juan*, it was the producer, David Chambers, who finally flew to New York and said –

DJ: – get your act together.

RN: Not even that. He wanted to see what the problem was and he knew we should work together. He never pushed it and was immensely fair. He presented each of us with a great deal of respect, which is what we were not seeing in the other person.

On the other hand, it can be a producer who pulls a project apart, which brings me to my involvement in a musical called *King*. I was asked to do a whole new book for this musical about Martin Luther King which was going into rehearsal in London in just two weeks. It had already been cast, the songs were all set and it had been designed. I agreed to do it for lots of reasons, one of which was I thought it could be a heroic show – something positive – and I felt this would be a nice thing to do. I certainly felt that Martin Luther King was a true hero.

When I was first asked, I said, 'Why don't you want a black writer?' And the producers said, 'We had black writers but it doesn't matter. We want you.' I started to stew a little and said, 'OK, but I'm not going to work unless I get a letter signed by all the producers and the collaborators, the people who wrote the music and the lyrics, saying that they want me.' It's the most obvious thing, because there were a number of different producers and a number of collaborators and they promised me I would have that.

Weeks went by. I wrote and wrote. There were excuses why I didn't have that letter and then I finished the first act. I refused to give them the second because that was my last bit of leverage to get this letter and then I was told that the letter couldn't be written because two people wouldn't sign it. So here I was after having done a whole new book to find out that I had a producer and a collaborator who refused to sign a letter to say they support my writing the show, at which point I went to the producers who did support me and said, 'I want out, because all I see is pain and trouble down the road. Please take my name off of it. Take my work. Do whatever you want. Do it and let me go home.' They told me to stay and said they would support me to the end.

To get to the lowest of the low points of this adventure, Mrs Martin Luther King disowned the project on the basis of a white person having written the book. Maya Angelou, the lyricist, disowned the show because I was white. Great pressure was put on me to work with a black writer – incredible pressure – and I agreed to work with anyone, if they told me what was needed and if we could get the best person to help. But until I was given notes about what was wrong with what I had written, I didn't want to just start hiring people, especially just because that person was black. Then I was told that I would never have to meet the black writer. That person could stay away; they just needed the name of a black writer. The whole thing seemed anathema.

It all came to a head at a company meeting called by the producers where Graham Vick, the director, and I were told our case was going to be supported. Graham and I were in the same boat and were extraordinarily close and we supported each other to the end. At this point, the producers, instead of saying, 'We support Richard and his book,' said that they wanted to make a big push to get the statement of Mrs Martin Luther King reversed, to have her support our musical. To do that changes would have to be made in the book and they called upon the black members, especially the black American members, of the company to tell me, Richard, what should be changed.

This was unbelievable. Graham stood up and said, 'This is a wonderful book. No changes will be made unless Richard makes them. He has been open from day one to talk to anyone.' We stuck together and we both left the show at the same time.

DJ: Do you think in retrospect you got warning signals much earlier which you ignored because you were keen to pursue that particular project?

RN: Without a doubt any white writer would have had that problem. And, in fact, any black writer who wished to take

Martin Luther King as anything but a plaster-cast saint. But I was naïve enough and hopeful enough to think at the beginning that what the producers were telling me was true. The signals were a little slow in coming, but after all most of the producers were white, the composer was white, the director was white. It didn't seem to me that a book writer on this project being white was so peculiar.

DJ: The producer's great talent is to have enough enthusiasm for the project to pick the right team for it or to actually pick up and run with a piece that is brought to him, to fund it adequately, to run the financial side of the production – not indulgently, strictly, but with fairness – and to say, 'How can I help?' Mel Brooks did that superbly with me, Sam Spiegel more confrontationally. But there are very few producers like that. It's a very challenging job. It should be a proud profession but it has got itself a very bad name because of the number of amateurs who fly under that flag.

RN: Anyone can be a producer.

DJ: You could argue that anyone can be a director, but I think you get sussed out a lot sooner if you can't direct.

RN: Mostly you need to be hired to be a director or, if you're a playwright, you need to have your play picked. If you're a producer, you just call yourself a producer and you start making phone calls.

DJ: There are areas of barbarism out in the jungle that we both have had to deal with and a lot of the time you can deal with it if you hold your ground and don't panic, but it's exhausting and it's boring. Getting the artistic thing right is a tough enough struggle without having to deal with kindergarten politics of that sort. I mean, they're not kindergarten, they're lethal, but the mentality behind them is kindergarten, and that's tough. It's particularly tough in the final, vulnerable stages of rehearsal, when people start trying to 'judge' the production.

RN: I think once the playwright agrees that the aesthetic battles – the discussions of the *play* – are held between the playwright and the director in private, then the playwright is, in effect, passing along certain amounts of aesthetic power to the director.

The director must not then 'go public' and begin turning to producers and saying, 'I've had it. I've tried to convince the writer what should be done to his play, now you try.' If the director is not going to do that, then I think the playwright must have the confidence to say that any concerns about the production or the process of the production that the playwright has will be dealt with between the director and the playwright and will not be taken to a third or fourth party. I think it's a relationship that is best worked on in private, and that's, maybe, a radical thought.

DJ: Do you mean, as opposed to in a conference with producers or as opposed to on the rehearsal floor?

RN: I think both, for different reasons. I think not in conference with the producers, because I think producers by their nature will look out for their own fiefdoms and their own power and will enjoy their own input. If they see a split between the director and the playwright, they – some, many – will exploit that for their own position and that is detrimental to the process and creates a confused and somewhat paranoid atmosphere.

DJ: I know with David Mercer that he had friends who would come to previews and give comments on individual performances or maybe even lighting effects and, equally, people like Peter Hall would say things. If I disagreed with the comments, I wouldn't be bothered to raise them, but if I thought there was some validity then I would go to David and say, 'I don't know what we should make of this, but this is being fed through. Do you think we should address this, or not?'

RN: Of course. I don't mean that.

DJ: I'm saying that protection against everyone out there saying anything bad is destructive.

RN: I agree. What I mean is, if you argue and explain why something should be a certain way with the director and you don't include in those discussions other people, then you're not having to protect your ass. If the two of you are saying, 'Yes, we can work it out this way or that way,' and it's not working out, then the two of you should stick together to sort it out. If at that point the director says, 'I don't get it. Producer, you talk to the writer,' then the playwright is no longer in a partnership with his play, and it's a very, very, very common situation.

I don't want to be in charge or to get into a group argument of trying to explain things with producers or even with actors. I'm distrustful of my explanations of my own work – of even descriptions of my own work. You once heard me describe to a group of actors Act III of *Rip Van Winkle* and I confused every single person in the room.

If two people have formed a business partnership, they don't hide bad news from each other. They share it. The most important thing is that they share the dilemma and not call up someone else down the road.

DJ: I agree. It's very interesting, the question of deference, of the power balance. I think the only example where I've said to a writer, 'I'm sorry, I will not accept this any more,' was on *The Island of the Mighty*. To me the writer is the conscience of the production. That doesn't mean to say that in terms of how I deal with the actors, how I deal with the politics of the producers, etc., I won't go on my own way. I will use my authority and power as a director.

Maybe during rehearsal it will only be every third day that I'll turn to the writer and say, 'So, what do you think? Are we moving in the right direction?' I don't know that I could defer to the extent of saying, 'I only want to do with the show absolutely everything that you want,' because in a genuine partnership the director will be realizing the writer's vision in the performances that he gets or in the design that he wraps around them. Hopefully, the director will not only realize the playwright's vision, but add a little bit extra, so that out of working together you can arrive at something beyond the initial expectation.

RN: I think more than that . . . it's not even a question of having something a little extra. It's a question of the difference between a flower and a bud. One is very beautiful and one is not necessarily very beautiful and they're very different, but one couldn't exist without the other, and one, if it's successful, becomes the other.

There's an incredible amount of input that a director has beyond the element of revisions. There's nothing richer for a playwright than the discussion of the play, in the right way and in the right world. When we were going to do *Two Shakespearean Actors* on Broadway, I had a conversation with the director, Jack O'Brien, who was concerned about a scene. It's always been problematic – the Washington Irving scene – and he just said, he said it the right way to me, 'Richard, it's simply not hot enough for me. The play has got to be getting hot at that time. Can you make it hotter?' And I think, 'Great! I see. He should be angrier.' That's a good way of talking to me, because one's talking about the engine of the play and what one's feeling.

*

Length is something both reviewers and producers
confuse with time. *Hamlet* is too long. So is *Don
Giovanni*. So, sometimes, is life.

John Osborne

DJ: When the play gets into previews it is really an exciting
time because a production takes megaleaps equivalent to
almost a week's rehearsal between each preview. I'm very
conscious of how many previews I've got and of trying to
give the company a specific objective for each night to deal
with the various areas of the play. I'm not alarmed when you
hit the down performance on the third or fourth preview.

In preview a director makes a personal judgement about
how the evening is going overall. In a sense, and certainly for
the first three previews until you've got the show almost to
where you want it to be, the judgement has to be almost
entirely yours alone.

The toughest thing to tell actors, especially if they've gone
on a roll with a preview audience after it's been a bit sticky in
rehearsal and they've begun to play out to the house a bit too
much, is that they have lost the story focus. It's not so much
hard to give the note but for them to take and believe it.
They will say, 'But it was great last night, and they laughed
so much, and my friends enjoyed it.' To which I reply, 'Yes,
but the performance will be like a rose that becomes full-
blown too soon and over-blown in the end.'

Is that a time when, if the company doesn't want to hear
that from a director, they'll come to the author and say,
'What do you think? We thought it was great last night but
David feels it was indulgent'?

RN: They may, but the playwright's going through something
at that time as well, and there is a bonding with the director
again because of another mutual need. The first few previews
are a very dangerous time. The frustration for the playwright
is that the director is honing what the playwright considers to
be maybe relatively small matters, while for the playwright

the important fact is that the meaning of the play is confronted with an audience for the first time.

DJ: Yes. Do those 150 or 700 people or whatever understand?

RN: You watch a director begin to worry about light cues and blockings so that the people in Row Q can see while for the first time since the first read-through, you, the playwright, are having megathoughts about the play. I'm only thinking of broad strokes and the director, by and large, is thinking fine strokes.

DJ: I don't entirely agree with that. I do think it's true that for the first two previews at least sixty, or maybe seventy, per cent of my notes will be technical. But it doesn't mean I'm not aware of other things. That is the enormous excitement and curiously I find that I am very detached and surgeon-like. I can sit in an audience and sense whether they're getting restless, whether the comedy is working, whether there is the absolute stillness.

With something that's as devastating as the post-torture scene in *Principia*, for instance, we both know there's a very fine line beyond which the scene can be over-stretched or self-pitying, and it's at the time when the scene is just ahead of the audience and they can't believe that anything that horrific could happen. They can't believe that these people are showing an extraordinary kind of bravery in coping with it while being broken.

The actor can come off and feel it went pretty well. Yet you sat in an audience and people fidgeted. If that scene's working, nobody is going to move. It's finding the way to achieve that which is to do with the incredible economy and authority of performance.

RN: As the director, you're continuing the process in a very logical way from rehearsal room to techs, to dress runs, to previews, and that is a growth. It may be a bit of a jump in certain places but it's a growth of 'Let's make it better, let's make it right.'

The playwright is a completely different animal. I'm working on a production, I'm involved with the details and how the whole flower is slowly opening, but, bingo, I'm suddenly interested in whether people think it is worthwhile. Do they have any idea of what the play is about? Does the meaning of the play in the broad sense matter to them?

So the basic ideas, which go back to almost the same discussions as the first meeting with the director, are now foremost again and the director isn't necessarily dealing with that.

DJ: A director is as concerned with 'Does it work?' and maybe more so with 'Does it work technically?' I don't mean in terms of lighting cues, etc., but my ability to manipulate the audience with this piece. Can I make them do the things which I think should happen to them at certain points? The playwright, I guess, is in a much more vulnerable state, thinking, 'Does anyone have the slightest interest in my story?'

RN: Exactly. As a writer, your goal is to convey something, to articulate something. The process of rehearsal is one where you are articulating to and with the people who are then going to present your story. But the final thing is you, your story, your play and what is being understood or appreciated, or not being understood or appreciated. One is very alone at that point.

When *Between East and West* was done at Yale, the first preview was the worst first preview I've ever had. We did the title projections with two slide projectors that would fade in and out, and after the first projection a bulb blew so that only every other scene had a title. 'Before' is the title of one scene and the title of the next is 'And After'. In this case there was no 'Before' so the whole thing made little sense and this play, which I worried about being too refined, became I thought clearly pretentious in its meaning.

This was said afterwards and I kept replying, 'It's because a bulb blew.' And everyone simply said, 'No, no, we understand that. We're from the theatre, but that's not what we're saying.' I came under pressure to rewrite but I didn't and the play with both bulbs working seemed quite moving.

DJ: I understand that, but those technical things, the performances, whatever, are all the instruments of communicating your meaning and until those instruments are all operating at 100 per cent efficiency, the meaning will not be 100 per cent communicated.

RN: I understand that and that's the dilemma.

DJ: I don't think any production I've done works for at least three previews and, curiously, at that stage I never feel it's my production on the line. When I've got it to as good as I can get it, then I'm on the line, but not before that.

In America you're talking almost always of a much longer preview period, which has advantages and also great dangers because everyone can start to pass comment, whereas in England I used to be very happy with the old rhythm of three previews and hit the press. I'm uncomfortable with more than five previews because I know that with five, like a sports coach, I can deliver the best performances across the board on the press night.

It's much more difficult when you're in previews for, let's say, eleven days. The actor is so much in charge of what he's doing on the stage that I think there's a point of diminishing return where you can affect what is happening. Probably I just need to learn a new work method.

RN: The one problem with the short group of previews in a repertory like the RSC is that you get into a rhythm where rewrites are not logical but cuts are.

DJ: You do not have the time for the rewrites to be written, rehearsed and tried in front of audiences. It's something I've never had the chance to do. When we did *Rip Van Winkle*, we didn't have time for that.

RN: That would be fine by me if everyone went into the first preview with an agreement that it is a frozen script and we're going to make it work. However, there's one tool still available that can be used in a run of short previews, which is the hatchet, and that's a very, very dangerous tool to wield with a new play.

DJ: Much more exercised in the States than in England, or have you had similar experiences in England?

RN: I've had similar.

DJ: In America it seems the most common reaction to almost anything in preview, whether it's working or not, is one of panic. There is a basic lack of confidence – a lot of fear in the air – which is very difficult to overcome. With all that flak going on or knowing that it's going to hit you, how much can you learn from sitting out among the audience?

RN: It's tricky. I think continuity with the audience is important. We've all seen an audience stand up and cheer, and this happens in the United States a great deal more than in England, and you sit there and wonder why they're doing this. We all know that the buttons of an audience can be pushed in a certain way. So I find that it helps if I can know the audience. I can now gauge in England a little better than I can gauge in America whether things are coming across or not.

There's an old rule on Broadway that you can tell if the audience liked a show or not by how many programmes they left on the floor. The more they left, the less they liked it.

DJ: That's a very interesting measuring stick.

RN: The programmes are free. In England everyone takes them because they –

DJ: – they paid good money.

RN: Interference at previews is a very, very difficult thing and the relationship of the director and the playwright must be so, so tight to handle it well. In a very small production of a play of mine the set that was delivered was poorly built. We had a run-through and the artistic director apparently didn't think it was going very well. I heard this not directly but through the workshops when they were told not to rebuild the set because it wasn't worth the money. What do you do?

DJ: Difficult.

RN: Very difficult. If the show didn't work, it didn't work, but you can't make that decision after a run-through. I felt a trust had been broken by the theatre by not delivering what had been promised and the only way we got the set rebuilt was because the director and I were very, very together.

In another case, the artistic director of the theatre was not involved in the selection of my play for a whole number of reasons, and therefore didn't really support it. The play was a farce and a very difficult play to get on so we were anxious to know what the first audience response would be. The artistic director usually addressed the first preview audience and he stood up and said, 'Tonight, as you know, is a work in progress. You've all been here before. Some things will work, some things will not happen and people could stop if they have to. But I just want to tell you the old story of the vaudevillian who was dying in a hospital in New Jersey. His friend said, "Joey, Joey, how are you?" And Joey replied, "Well, dying's easy, comedy's hard."' The artistic director then wished them a good evening and my farce began.

DJ: Oh, my God!

RN: After that preview, there was a post-mortem, with the artistic director and staff saying why this play was a mistake and why we shouldn't be doing it. And we still had another ten days of previews to go. That's a great, great error and a great confusion, and again a trust broken with the theatre. If they choose to do the play, they must support it at least up through opening night. That's the minimum.

I've mentioned *Accidental Death of an Anarchist* already. Well, at one preview the producer, Alex Cohen, poked his finger in my chest and demanded some rewrites he'd asked for. There were five jokes that he thought were in poor taste and he'd wanted those out of his production.

DJ: He was upset by them?

RN: He'd told me he did not produce plays with such language. I'd laughed. I couldn't believe it. I mean he's produced incredible things and this didn't make sense. I'd looked at it and out of the five, three were going to go anyway because they didn't work and two of them were very funny, so I was going to argue for them. We hadn't had time to make any changes in the script, so just as the first act was coming down, Cohen says, 'I want to talk to you.' We went out into the street, he started to push me and say, 'Son, if you know what's good for you, those cuts will be made by tomorrow night.' This was in the middle of the intermission on West 44th Street and I ended up heaving my script into the middle of the street and telling him he was a son of a bitch. That wasn't a very healthy way to do theatre either.

DJ: Returning to a happier note in relation to previews and the director–dramatist relationship, do you find it valuable or useful to come to note sessions so you know what the director is saying to the cast?

RN: I have learned not to go to note sessions. That's a new

thing. I think because they deal with minutiae, they're probably one of the most boring elements of the production for me and if my mind is full of something else, I'm not throwing off a lot of positive energy. I'll go sometimes to throw in my solidarity but often I'm not in a cheerleader mood. However, what's most important to me is finding those times with the director when we can go through our notes.

Occasionally there have been times when the director says, 'Come to notes and explain that.' And that's fine. If there's a warm feeling we've developed then that's great. But it's here once again that the contract and the trust are very, very important. Your disappointments or doubts can be the same as the director's, but the trust is not to bring those to anyone except the director.

Even though the director may not want to spend time with the playwright at that point, that's when he must. More than at any other time, it's a moment for not just five minutes but a couple of hours of sitting down and saying, 'Are you sure, are you confident?' It's when a million doubts rage and they're all shot at oneself. For all the cheerleading, the role is slightly changed.

DJ: Actors are really smart in terms of learning from an audience, but like all of us they like to be liked so that's the only danger area. Also they are as insecure as you or I and therefore if they go through an evening where there is no feedback at all, they panic. You have said, 'That audience was really rapt with attention. Did you hear the response at the end?' I would rather have that than manic laughter through act one and then a dying lack of interest as the play goes on.

RN: This is where the pay-off of sitting in those rehearsals comes in. I've forced myself, and now I end up enjoying going around at the end of every preview to the . . .

DJ: . . . to the dressing room.

RN: . . . to the actors.

DJ: Do you still find that tough?

RN: Not any more.

DJ: But you used to. Was that just shyness or you just didn't know what to say?

RN: I didn't know what to say. My mind was full of other things. What I've found is that I just say it's good. I just speak my enthusiasm which I really, really feel and if they know me well enough, they can judge my levels of enthusiasm. What I'm showing is the support. I'm saying, 'We're in this together.'

It's important because there can be a swell of people who want to cut loose from the production. There are all kinds of people coming around saying, 'The play's great, the direction's bad,' or 'The play's great, the actors are bad.' Or they're going to the actor and saying, 'You're great, but I don't think this play is any good.' And to the director, 'Oh, you've really made the most of this one.' (*Both laugh.*)

But at that point, there's a feeling that the playwright doesn't have any function any more. But I think you and I have proved that the playwright still does function once the show is up.

DJ: As the unifier, because the director gets back very late to the wood from living among the trees, and there are so many trees to be dealt with.

RN: The playwright offers a sense of the wholeness of it all. If things are not working, this unifying sense comes into play in changes, in rewrites, in cuts or whatever. In the perfect world the relationship with the director comes back to a mutual need somewhere in the preview period before the press come in and the reviews come out.

DJ: Occasionally I've got a good review as a director where critics have trashed the play and I don't understand that. I have always felt that any play I was directing has something outstanding in it, was something I wanted to be doing, and it makes me angry when there's a misinformed attempt to separate out the two contributions. I try to read all the critics. I don't do it as much as I used to. My job is primarily one of communication and I want to know, did I communicate the story in its full resonance?

The critics are only part of the equation and what I sense in an audience night after night is also part of it. But I want to know how the piece was perceived by the critics. In England it's easier to do because you know that it's not going to be all bad, hopefully, and there are many different points of view.

Every now and again you get a review which talks about things in your production that you weren't aware you put in, but you can see are there, and that's exciting. A critic can occasionally give you a new perspective on something you've done. I guess that's why if they say this was a brilliant production of a poor bit of material, then I think I've fucked up because clearly they're seeing something which they're not understanding.

Do you find critics easy to read, or do you put off reading them for a while?

RN: I read them right away. And they have a great impact, not influence.

DJ: . . . he said, scraping himself off the wall. (*Laughter.*)

RN: The reviews I've had in America until the early nineties have been very negative. There have been some good ones and some supporters or I couldn't have gotten my plays on otherwise. Some major critics have not liked my plays. But, on the other hand, there's a positive side to critics. In 1986 when we did *Principia* I had been very, very low. I didn't think my work was making sense to a lot of people and I just couldn't see the light at the end of the tunnel of building a career and doing the work with confidence.

I felt that I had been building a career to a point where I could write on a large scale and take on the theatre in a way that very few people had prepared themselves to do. But I never found myself in a position where I could let myself go. I just kept being thwarted. When *Principia* opened in New York early in 1986 it got nice reviews but some not so nice – 'he's a second-rate David Hare' kind of reviews.

I remember going to get the papers after the opening in London and I remember picking up the *Guardian* to read Michael Billington, and I remember standing against a wall and the first thought that came to me was, 'So, I'm not crazy.' The power of it all was just amazing because it was such a relief. It wasn't satisfaction. It wasn't like, 'Oh, boy! I got a hit show.' It was, 'I'm not mad. And what I'm trying to do was understood and someone articulated this back to me, and I read it.'

Often, the positive reviews I've read didn't articulate it back to me. Maybe they understood, but they didn't describe it back. But here was someone who had. And then there were many other reviews of that production that did it as well, but it was Michael Billington with that show, and other shows since, who has given me a focus and a respect for criticism, so that I can now pick up a review without the trepidation that I once had.

That production and those reviews gave me a career in England and a career at the RSC and a home for which I was ready. I was ready to expand. It gave me hope.

DJ: It's such a public forum you have to perform in as a playwright. You went through ten years of not being understood, or worse. It wasn't just that they were being critical or abusive, it's just that they didn't get what you were doing.

Both for the director and the writer – I can't remember

who first said this – one of the most important qualities to have is stamina. You have to stay in the ring for the full fifteen rounds. It never crossed my mind that *Principia* was anything but an extraordinary play. It just demolished me initially. If I'd known how much was hanging on that production – you told me since that it was your last pitch and you felt that if it had not gone well in England, your life would have changed direction – then I would have found that an alarming responsibility. What was recognized by the English critics was the sheer authority of the piece, the conviction about what you were doing and the individuality of the tone of the voice. Maybe in those years of misunderstanding and rejection, there was a way of your finding a voice.

SEVEN

Feeling Hurt and Betrayed?:
the Future Relationship

> You should choose your theatre like you choose a
> religion. Make sure you don't get into the wrong
> temple.
>
> *George Devine's advice to his godson who wanted
> to enter the theatre*

RN: One thing that helps a playwright keep going is a continued relationship with a director. So, what do you think has
made a number of British playwrights split from their directors, or vice versa?

DJ: Well, I don't see a single production as a marriage. A
single production is, maybe, a love affair; maybe it gets as far
as an engagement. The marriage comes when you and the
writer begin to feel that there is a partnership there which
should become longer term. It becomes a real partnership if
the writer always sends the most recent piece of work to the
director, even if the director may not be the person to direct
it. It happened to me relatively late on in my career with
Harold Pinter from *Langrishe, Go Down* at the end of the
seventies. But now when he writes something he sends it to
me, as he did with *Mountain Language*.

I feel very proud that you send me your new work when
it's finished. You're always very tactful about it, but to know
that the material is shared is part of our permanence, which is
very important to me. I don't know if there is a stage when a
director who has a particular affinity with a writer has to
stand aside. It's very tough for the director to accept that but
it may be important that other people get to work on that
playwright's work. One of the most feared and, by some

people, disliked of British directors, John Dexter, did extra-ordinary work with both Peter Shaffer and Arnold Wesker. He had a terrier-like toughness that got hold of material that maybe was a little chaotic and kicked it into shape and gave it a voice that was partly his work. Why he and Shaffer stopped working together, I don't know. With Arnold I think there was a feeling that everyone behaved as if Dexter was the only person that could direct his stuff and he want-ed to show that he could achieve with other people. Plus Arnold wanted to direct himself. Those are things that can happen.

David Mercer had an extraordinary round of television productions with a very, very good director called Don Taylor. Don came from a London working-class background, David from Yorkshire. After several shows he said to David, 'What you have to write next is . . .' and at that point, some-thing in David said, 'Wait a minute. I'm being taken over.' It's the great danger of marriage, where suddenly one partner starts to get too dominant or starts to assume things in a relationship rather than earning them. You begin to expect that, of course, your next play by your writer who you're so attached to will be sent to you.

I remember a sense of extraordinary pain when David Mercer had been talking to me about a new play of his called *Flint*. We'd had one of those classic lunches where he'd told me he'd got an idea, and then he said it was nearly finished and then he rang me up: 'Something terrible has happened,' he said. 'The play's finished, but I've given it to this new production company. They rang me up out of the blue and said they were starting this new company and they really wanted to do a play of mine.'

I had no right to feel hurt and betrayed, but I did. I mean, extremely so. The only other time this happened to me, and that was with a writer that I did not have a relationship with, was with Trevor Griffiths. I was really knocked out by *Occupations*, which Buzz Goodbody did an extraordinary production of. I was in charge of the London end of the

RSC, and Trevor is a volatile writer to have in rehearsals, so I stayed very close to the production, partly to protect Buzz a bit and partly because I was so excited by it and thought it was so important. I talked to Trevor about what he wanted to do next, and he talked to me about this play he wanted to write called *The Party* about the Socialist Labour League. I think we had three lunches to discuss his progress.

Meanwhile he was under commission to the National Theatre to do a play about Kronstadt and the Battleship Potemkin. The fourth lunch came, and he said, 'I finished *The Party* and Ken Tynan insisted on seeing it.' 'But you're not writing that on commission for them,' I said. 'I got stuck with that one,' he replied, 'and it turns out that the terms of my commission mean that I have to give them whatever play I've finished.' I foolishly thought, 'We're OK. Olivier is still running the National. He won't touch this piece of very advanced left-wing propaganda.' But, of course, the clever old fox saw in it the last great part of his acting career and went for it.

I don't know how you resist being proprietorial. I think you really have to address yourself quietly as a director and say you have no right to be proprietorial beyond a point. The most difficult phase of our relationship was the time when you had stuff ready to go, I wanted to do it, and I couldn't make myself available to do it, and I couldn't understand why you wouldn't wait. I know I was wrong about that. But I think I am human and, however annoying or frustrating it was for you, it was a compliment to how highly I thought of you that I wanted to do the play.

When you look historically at intensive periods of co-operation between director and writer, they don't seem to get reforged later. The original firing of the two talents may last a long or a short time but you can't restore the old intensity if the relationship is fractured. With William Gaskill and Edward Bond, more than anything, more than the way he did the plays, it was just his unshakeable belief in Edward's work that was so crucial. Again, it's a little like the Wesker problem.

Edward is set on directing his own work and I don't quite know why this becomes an obsession with a writer. Peter Nichols has talked about wanting to direct his own work and has done so. Harold Pinter has, as you know. I don't know whether it's to do with a sense that the playwright is the only person who can understand the play, which is the message one's getting from Bond and Wesker.

There are only three things that will really screw up the relationship. One is if a play comes along which the director, in the writer's view, misunderstands and distorts. The second is if the playwright says, 'I've written a new play, but I'm not going to ask you to direct it,' or 'I would ask you to direct it, but unless you can do it tomorrow, you're not going to direct it.' I think that's a difficulty when the two careers are not going in harness. The third, though I think it can be ridden, is when the playwright comes up with a play which the director does not truly admire as much as he's admired the earlier work. I talked about this in relation to David Mercer. The play was a kind of Shavian political debate with Orton overtones, and I saw no way of staging it. It never did get staged and I think David was very distressed for a while that I didn't respond to him, but we came through that.

This has happened on two occasions with us. One I've been always fairly honest about is *An American Comedy*. I just knew I was tone deaf to that. I could tell there was something happening there, but I didn't know what to do with it. With *Some Americans Abroad* I was badly wrong about it when I first read it, not that it ever became likely that I could do it. I probably made the mistake of feeling this was a slightly easy target satire. I couldn't see the underpinning of human loneliness and despair or the fact that the comedy is much deeper, more rooted.

That's what I admired enormously about Roger's production in both England and America. I thought it gave the play a stature which I had not discerned in it at first. I don't think there's anything else of yours that I've read that I haven't wanted passionately to direct. What I've learned to live with is the fact that I'm not available to direct all of it and that you have to have other directors. One's only fear then is will the playwright ever want you to do something again or is that a phase of his life that he's gone through?

RN: It's hard when you're having different careers and it's very difficult in the movie world, to tie yourself down a year in advance for a two-month period to do a stage play. But I think we'll always keep coming back to each other. We have a marriage, but a promiscuous one. (*Laughter.*)

DJ: Just like a marriage that turns in on itself too much, it begins to dry up if there are no juices coming from other sources. Interestingly, just a couple of years before David Mercer died, I went back into television to run 'Play of the Month' where I could take my pick of classic plays to be presented and I was adamant that I wanted some modern classics in there. I included *Flint*. By that time I had enough distance from it not to feel the need to direct it myself and I asked Peter Wood to do it, who is a quite extraordinary television director. I felt that that particular relationship had found its full circle in due course.

RN: It's a very tricky relationship at this point in the marriage because it's very important for one side not to take advantage or take the other for granted. If either of you think, 'I've already got this partnership. Therefore, I don't have to develop the relationship on this play,' then that's a mistake. Second productions are very interesting because in the first production, especially if it's going well, everyone's on their best behaviour and then with the second one, one person's shorthand can be another person's slight.

DJ: Yes, I know. I think we were very lucky to have five years between our first and second productions.

RN: We did *Rip Van Winkle* and then we went off in different directions, and then we came back.

There are playwrights looking at other playwrights and saying, 'That guy's got a good relationship. That director's doing his work or getting her work done so I'm going to cosy up to him.' You also see it in directors who say, 'There's a playwright. I could poach him.'

For me, our relationship is basic to what I do and how I've grown. Peculiarly, the most successful relationships I've had with directors have been with foreign directors, and specifically English directors, even before I'd had my work done in England. You and John Madden – both English. Since then, Trevor Nunn, Roger Michell, Graham Vick, John Caird. Jack O'Brien is the exception in that he's American. It's quite a range of people. Each one drawing something from me. It's a good growth, just as you wouldn't want every movie you made written by Hugh Whitemore or Richard Nelson.

DJ: There are other writers that I would love to do more with, like Edward Bond, but you begin to think of certain writers as out of bounds if they have a regular relationship with another director. I was asked to do one of the three Bond fables for an anti-apartheid evening in 1970 and I said, 'Why haven't you asked Bill Gaskill?' I said I would feel very bad if I didn't know that either Edward specifically didn't want Bill or that Bill had been asked and couldn't or didn't want to do it. Edward rang me back himself and said, 'I just wanted a change on this one. Bill knows I'm doing it. It's not a big deal. I'd like you to do it.'

I would love to direct with Sam Shepard sometime, but I'm not sure that would be a marriage made in heaven. I admire his work enormously and I think I understand even the difficult side of it. But he has such a developed persona now . . .

RN: He's directing his own work.

DJ: It's interesting to think about the author as director and how the director can take the writer for granted. It's summed up in a way by that hilarious story in Simon Gray's memoirs of a production directed by Harold Pinter where Harold cuts Simon's photograph out of the programme because Simon is only the writer. (*Laughter*.) And now Simon, having done a couple of productions in America that have been successful, wants to direct his own stuff. I'm trying to make sure that the role of director, which I think is going to fall into abeyance in the year 2000, sticks in there until then. Do you ever think you'd like to direct?

RN: Not when I've been –

DJ: – in sane mind. (*Laughter*.)

RN: No – with really good directors. There were two productions where I thought I could do better. Not that I could do well, but I could do better. And that's a very dangerous thought. I probably still harbour a few thoughts of trying to direct a classic play, out of curiosity. But never my own work. We've talked about what that playwright–director relationship is and how important and how complex and how pitched it must be within a rehearsal process and how lonely one could be without it. The playwright/director must feel very lonely.

DJ: Because you have no one to talk to but yourself.

RN: And you could do a disservice to both jobs very easily.

DJ: There's a lack of relaxation in the relationship between the playwright/director and the actor because the actor feels daunted by dealing with the playwright and director in one person. I've had the much less difficult experience of directing a writer acting in his own work. I directed Harold in *Langrishe, Go Down* but that was one day of filming. I also directed him in *Old Times* and that was made possible by Harold's meticulous understanding of and ability to express the nice-ties. He called me in a week before rehearsal and said, 'You have to understand. I am an actor on the rehearsal room floor. You must not feel any sense of having to defer to me or that I necessarily know the right answers. I am an actor, very out of practice, struggling to do this difficult role.'

We got to the second day of rehearsal and – I don't know if you carry your plays in your head, but I don't think Harold found it that hard to learn the part – he was starting to get off the book early. He was nervous and was machine-gunning his way through pages where there were a lot of Pinter pauses. Harold had already told me that he was bored by the whole business of pauses. 'Use them if you want to,' he said. 'Neglect them if you want. I don't care any more about pauses. It's not the important thing in my work.'

I felt very strongly he was jumping over things and I said, 'Harold, it's very exciting what you're doing with that page, but I don't think it's quite what the author intended.' He said, 'What do you mean?' I said, 'I don't think that the person who wrote this text meant it to be played quite that way.' He said, 'Really? Will you explain that?' I said, 'Well, we know the pauses are not sacred, but I think what's going on here is that he is having a problem in making the jump to saying the next thing. I think here he is stopping because if he opens his mouth, he's going to scream and lose his temper and he doesn't want to do that in public in front of these two women. I think there are a lot of events here which you're skipping over.' He said, 'You think that's what the author would feel?' I said, 'I'm certain of it.' He said, 'In that case, I will change my performance.'

That was how we conducted the whole rehearsal from then on. I would always refer to this figure of the author as someone 'out there' who in the end had to be deferred to. And I was the person who knew what the author intended better than Harold did. He played this game quite beautifully, but the problem was that Liv Ullman was in hysterics with laughter at the whole thing. She couldn't believe these two crazed men were talking in this way. But it got the results.

RN: That's a terrific relationship – you protecting the author from the author who's now not the 'author' but an 'actor'. However, one of the routes to divorce is when the relationship gets to the point where one party says, 'I know better than you.' Peter Nichols has had some highly publicized situations where plays of his were done in ways that he had not intended but they have been successful. However, I see the most important thing in my writing life as the ability to get up in the morning and get to my desk and begin to work. I dread something getting in the way. If someone came along and said, 'I'll make you rich. I'll make the show you're working on a big, big success. You'll be praised as the greatest writer but the terms are it will not be what you intended.'

DJ: The Mephistopheles offer –

RN: – I would refuse that offer very, very clearly and I would refuse it without any question, any doubt. But it's very hard to refuse unless you're focused on a longer-range growth of your work.

DJ: People had very different intentions when *Poppy* was produced. I don't think Peter was averse to being enormously successful, but I think his main priority was that if the show was being done by the RSC it would be done the way he, the author, *wanted* and then could be enormously successful too. Getting the show right was more important to him than box office returns, and that's where he felt let down.

RN: This delicate balance of a relationship is a marriage. It is not that one person is the parent and one is the child. It can't ever develop that way. If it's not worked at and thought through and maintained then one side is going to feel very used or taken advantage of or the subject of the other.

DJ: Has a director ever treated you as if you were a dead writer?

RN: In which way? Has he ever wanted me dead? Ever wanted to kill me? One or two, I think. Or did he simply ignore me?

DJ: As if you didn't exist. The text was there. It was not of importance that someone was around who had written that text and therefore might have views on its meaning and the best way of presenting it.

RN: No, apart from the director in Los Angeles who was in a state of nervous breakdown. I don't know how you could ever do that, because as a human being – me – standing there in rehearsal, how much rudeness can you take before exploding?

DJ: There are quite a few directors who would not allow you to be in rehearsal.

RN: The normal contract provides for access to rehearsal. Though I treat that access as an invitation to be a guest of the director, I would be loath to have someone say . . .

DJ: 'I don't want you here,' and then insist on it.

RN: We must look beyond the particular project in front of us, otherwise we're not really artists and I think that's uniquely what the true director–playwright relationship can be. It can be a spine for artistic growth.

DJ: I think it's personal rather than career orientated in the sense that the miracle for a director is to find the playwright whose preoccupation, whose subject matter, whose sense of character – above all, whose tone of voice – is, as I've said, like what you hope you might have written if you had been a writer. It's a rare quality. You direct lots of other dramatists whose work does not have this quality, and you understand them and you get a kick out of doing them, but it's not as immediately linked to the root of you.

What was strange was that there was a period, with Mercer and Gorky and Günter Grass – although I only did one of his plays, I was very close to his writing – when all the writers whose work I was presenting were big, rather bear-like, slightly clumsy, but very powerfully energized. Maybe I found in their work something that released in me all the things that were a little too cautious, a little too self-critical, a little too held-in. There was a panache about their work that was very releasing to me. They had an emotional openness, an honesty, a bravado that I aspired to and their plays – working on them – helped me to get some of those qualities into my work and, hopefully, my life.

This will sound extremely winsome I know but when I did the Gorky plays I felt so close to them that I did not consider him dead. I had a poster for *Enemies* with that face of his looking out and I used to go home after each preview and I would talk to it and ask, 'What do you think?' Just that contact, the sense of his presence, was very strong to me. Totally fanciful, but important.

RN: It's an extraordinary marriage and it's a uniquely twentieth-century one. You look at the history of the century's theatre and you can't ignore the partnerships: Granville Barker and George Bernard Shaw, Constantin Stanislavsky and Anton Chekhov, Elia Kazan and Tennessee Williams or Elia Kazan and Arthur Miller. You can go on. However, there are many exceptions, of course.

DJ: Some bitchy marriages in America that didn't all work.

RN: And they didn't last long.

DJ: Chekhov does not speak well of Stanislavsky a lot of the time.

RN: It doesn't have to be friendly; just two people who, if they understand the rules, can really push each other in the right way, a very healthy way as opposed to a negative way. It's a very symbiotic relationship, especially since the theatre has become technologically so advanced. It's not simply a group of actors sitting in a room, but it's about visions of the world and how they need to be done; in speed or in segments or whatever. There's a visual revolution and an audio revolution happening, and if you want to be a playwright in the twenty-first century you must incorporate this and let it grow within your work. You must be able to use theatre in all of its forms, and so the relationship with the director is essential for your growth. It's the director who is pushing those points, and so it's a necessary and a fantastic relationship that is the very heart and centre of twentieth-century theatre, of its success as well as its failure.

DJ: That's true. All those partnerships you cite were trail-blazing relationships. They were, in their own ways, revolutionary partnerships trying to change the perception of what theatre could and should be, and maybe it needs two people to make that breakthrough.

It's those partnerships that created a body of work that is still drawn on. Whereas, if you take someone like Piscator or Meyerhold – great directors, though not necessarily always working with scripts of enormous distinction – what they did was very important, but I don't know if it's any longer relevant. Curiously, the other work that has lasted is from the primary writer/director theatre innovator of our time, Bertolt Brecht.

RN: He successfully combined the skills of both. I have theatrical visions that are beyond the page but I'm not a director. It's my collaboration with the director that can build a new way of putting a play together, and it must happen with a director who's willing to confront new territory and risk new forms.

DJ: It suddenly occurs to me to wonder what would Strindberg's life have been like if someone had been there as his partner, his director, who really understood how to stage those last plays of his. Maybe he might have said occasionally, 'Draw in your horns a little,' or maybe he would have put them up on stage and made them work.

EIGHT

An Old Marriage: *Misha's Party*

It is a luxury to be understood.

Ralph Waldo Emerson

[In October 1991 I went to Moscow, having been 'matched' in a Russian–American writers' exchange programme with the Russian playwright, politician and journalist Alexander Gelman. The intention of the programme was to pair playwrights in the hope of engendering an interest in 'adapting' each other's plays for one's respective country. I arrived in Moscow with the more audacious intention of writing a play with Gelman from scratch. We worked for two weeks that October, then met again, months later, at the MacDowell Artists' Colony in New Hampshire; and then met once more in Moscow. *Misha's Party* is the result of that collaboration, which may appear even more quixotic when one knows that Gelman speaks no English and I no Russian. It was commissioned by the Royal Shakespeare Company and the Moscow Art Theatre, an historic first.

The play takes place in a hotel in Moscow which overlooks the Russian parliament during one night of the abortive 'August coup' of 1991.

Misha's Party had a staged reading, directed by David Jones, at the New York Public Library for the Performing Arts at Lincoln Center in March 1993. It premiered at The Pit, produced by the Royal Shakespeare Company, and directed by David Jones on 21 July 1993.

This conversation took place two mornings after the press night when most of the daily critics had published – a time of great vulnerability and touchiness. The initial reviews were not as favourable as we had expected, with Michael Billington's mixed review in the *Guardian* being especially disorienting for me as he had been my most understanding critic for years. RN]

*

The Morning After

RN: I'm disappointed so far with the reaction to the play – the critical reaction as opposed to the audience reaction. In terms of our book, as the director, what do you say to this bruised writer?

DJ: I offer enormous sympathy and I apologize for the obtuseness of the English critical fraternity. It's not a thing I usually feel about them. The state of drama criticism in England is generally pretty good and in America it's low, and in film criticism it's the other way round. What I find extraordinary is that they seem completely shuttered off from the experience happening in front of them. They clearly expected a play that was more serious, more political, and it seems to me absolutely clear to anyone with ears to hear and a heart to feel that this is a very human comedy. Those are the two crucial words.

What we get in the reviews is a very cerebral feeling that Mr Yeltsin offstage is under-written and these people are lunatically indifferent to the political events outside. No one is grasping the fact that one of the things the play is saying is exactly that. I think of the play as a major piece about the human condition, not about specific politics in Russia in 1991, and I would just advise the critics to look back historically. It's very Russian in that sense – Gorky did *Children of the Sun* at the time of the 1905 revolution and walked right around it. God knows what the critics said to Chekhov when he wrote *Uncle Vanya* because they would have seen it as sublimely irrelevant to Russia's main problems.

RN: What I'm feeling is what I dread most in life, which is to

be misunderstood. The play intentionally is extremely under-
written. The danger when you write the tip of the iceberg is
that some people won't believe there is anything underneath it.

I feel misunderstood in a political sense too. My work has
been moving towards looking at a world where there are large
events which are not created and controlled by individuals, a
world where there are no *great* individuals controlling *great*
events but where there are *great* events and there are lots of
individuals. The relationship between the two is fascinating.
It's at the centre of how I see the world and how I see my
future work.

Where I am lost right now is not so much looking back at
Misha's Party but looking forward; if this play is misunderstood, then other things I aim to write may also be
misunderstood.

The history that you and I have had together has charged
this production in an extraordinary way. There has been a
shorthand of working together, but you had an effect on the
writing in two ways. One, in the six or seven productions we
have worked on together and during the fifteen years we have
known each other, you have guided me in the direction of a
certain kind of writing. You've directed me towards someone
like Granville Barker, and in particular that last scene in *The
Marrying of Ann Leete*. You love so much the under-writing of
that scene, the sense of saying things and meaning other things
which is not only contemporary, like the dynamic of film, but
also reflects the way in which we live our lives. Two, in terms
of the growth of the production, the history that we've had
together allowed me to know that you knew there was an
iceberg under there and you were chipping away to find it.

DJ: My prime consideration always is to tell the story with its
own clarity and depth to an audience. I believe this is a
delicate, difficult, sensitive, elusive story which I think you as
writer, the actors as cast, I as director have told as well as it
can be told and I have never been so happy or proud of a
performance. On other occasions I might be racking my brain

saying, 'Where did I fail to get something over?', this time I've never felt more strongly that a group of people quite different from the preview audiences, who had no problem in responding to the play, saw it with previously formed agendas of what they thought this play should be about, and I think the problem is theirs not ours.

RN: Do you remember reading the play for the first time or hearing about the play for the first time?

DJ: I remember you talking to me about it quite a lot and quite a little. You were very secretive about how you were working with Alexander Gelman but you did talk about it. And I think, in a way, looking back I was probably rather less interested in it than I should have been. I said, 'Ah yes, Richard's writing that play in Russia, OK fine. It'll be finished one day. Maybe.' I certainly wasn't ringing up every day saying, 'How's the Russian play going?' and I was very thrilled when, as you usually do with a new piece of work, you sent it to me. I had learned a big lesson with *Some Americans Abroad* so I was ready when I read *Misha's Party* to see enormous things happening beneath that surface of apparent banalities. Naturally, I'm a sucker for anything Russian because of my background with Gorky, but there was a directness and an emotional fullness and a full-blooded humour about the characters, and a new expansiveness to the writing. I was very moved by the sense of two people – the very central thread of the play – at sixty looking back, deciding what their lives add up to, what could they pass on to other people, the difficulty of communication between generations, between parents and children; all that was very emotive so I knew it was an enormously rich play. Miraculously, it came at a time when it looked like I could free myself and I was very honoured when you and the RSC together asked me to do it.

RN: Could we talk about differences in expectations? Let me be bold. We had a reading of the play in New York and you had only two or three hours of rehearsal with an extraordinary cast. The first thing I saw David Jones do was count the chairs to make sure there were enough for the actors and enough for him but not for me. I thought, 'This is an extraordinary development in director's preparation. He doesn't want me at the table,' and I sat back and thought, 'What's this about?' To be honest, I was confused.

DJ: I'm at a loss for words. I hadn't realized that happened. It was a small table, quite hard to get everyone around, which I thought was a little foretaste of the play to come. I think, because it was a very pressurized afternoon, I may not have been at my most diplomatic but this was not a conscious or planned decision. I think quite often you think that I'm being machiavellian or manipulative or setting something up when it's just sheer absent-mindedness!.

I knew you had gone through experiences with at least two other major directors during the time since we had last worked together, some of those experiences had been good, some of them had been combative. I knew that you had flexed your muscles a great deal and were now very much your own man and were going to be coming into rehearsals with very strong opinions about what should happen. When I first read the play, as you know, I thought there were certain things that needed doing to it and until I really began to understand it I thought that at times it was over-minimalist, under-written and too oblique. When we talked about that you fought your corner very hard and in the end the only things we changed, as far as I can remember, were the beginning, and marginally – and I think it was not in terms of dialogue (or maybe there was one line added) but in terms of movement – the end of the play.

RN: The beginning of the play is a very interesting part of the collaboration.

DJ: Which Tim O'Brien has his share in.

RN: You wanted to know more about the background of the coup, exactly what was happening, very wisely seeing that in England people would be asking questions that weren't going to be raised by the play and needed to be dispensed with, concerns which some critics had this week. So you suggested projections and lured me and cajoled me by telling me how wonderfully I've used them in the past.

DJ: 'How could we have a Nelson play without projections?' I said.

RN: You flattered me towards this goal that you had and I didn't quite know how to do that because I just didn't know how they would fit.

Around the same time Tim brought the set model to show me, at his own expense. We all met in New York and we looked at the model and it was wonderful. However, in the model there was this stage at the back of the hotel restaurant and Tim said this was where cabaret performers or singers would perform but there weren't any in my play. Now whether Tim was pushing me or whether you were pushing me towards a stage singer I have no idea. Anyway, the thought dawned on me that there could be a singer. I wanted an ironic use of these titles and I suggested some kind of heroic Alexander Nevsky music but how do you make that ironic? The way to do it was immediately to follow with a Western pop tune and I chose 'Memory' – which would deflate the sense of history. The first three minutes of the play were rewritten and I think anyone would say they work really well.

DJ: It came out of the central design demands of the play. You presented Tim and me with an enormous play, sixty per cent of which takes place in an enormous restaurant with an enormous table, and then you have two scenes in bedrooms, two scenes in a hotel lobby and one in a bar, all this to take place in a very small theatrical space – The Pit. Tim and I shook our heads over this a great deal and you sent me a historic document in which you said, 'I don't think there's a problem on the design here. We don't need beds to indicate a bedroom. Those scenes can be done in space.' I did not show this to Tim, with whom I had to be very severe. He kept referring to the little inset scenes and I would say, 'They're not little inset scenes, they're forty per cent of the play.' Eventually we came up with a forum – like an Elizabethan inner stage almost. Tim wanted to integrate that into the restaurant, so he said that it could be a cabaret bandstand in the corner and he then said loudly one day, 'Maybe Richard would like to start the show with a song. It's always good to start a show with a song.' I said, 'I don't think this is quite the moment to suggest that to him. Let's just wait till he sees the set.' It was a marvellous evolution, very tactful and gentle on all sides.

RN: Now I learn that I was graciously led to make my own decision!

DJ: We were trying to stimulate your creative urges once again when you thought you had finished the work.

RN: There was a good bit more to rewrite in the first scene, which came through the reading with things not being clear; who people were, how the play begins. As you know, where a scene begins is profoundly important in my work. Very often a great deal of action has happened just before the scene and in the scene certain things are being played out. It's an element of my thinking that there are no beginnings, there are no ends, which is the same notion as there are no simple solutions, there are no answers. The world is a fluid place. So a dramaturgy, a structure, where things begin in the middle is a reaffirmation of the fluidity of how I see things. There were a few other very small changes and you wanted some extra material because you knew you had a staging problem which we never got to solve until well into rehearsal.

DJ: You mean the neo-improvised dialogue for the arrival of the main course, which proved to be one of the most difficult things to rehearse because of the actors having to pick up very fast cues and at the same time get all the food and plates in the right place at the right time.

RN: In terms of the playwright–director relationship, rehearsal this time was ninety-nine per cent relaxed and fantastic, because I felt that you understood. A slight exception was over these rewrites, the so-called ad libs. I had written dialogue that wouldn't be heard because it would be spoken at the same time, and I purposely wrote a kind of dialogue that didn't have to do with cues, that wasn't specific, that people could fill in any way and wouldn't have to worry about whether they had a plate or which plate. You reorganized it to find little scenes in each moment. I talked to you a couple of times and then just decided to stand back because I knew something interesting was happening but there was a time when I thought, 'If it should be lots of little scenes, I would have written lots of little scenes.'

DJ: What you gave me was total ad lib, improvisation, if you like, chaos. I don't mean that in a pejorative, just a descriptive, way. You didn't allocate the lines, just gave me twenty-five lines. I allocated them and made sense of them, maybe too much sense, but I do not believe the actors could have ad libbed from nowhere during that stuff arriving. I think it had to be an incredibly elaborate bit of choreography, which then had to be disguised again. But I agree, I took hold of something that you meant to be scatter shot, over-organized it and then began to break it down again.

RN: I didn't allocate the lines because it was a statement of a 'non-scene'. I've worked with directors who would have let the actors choose from those lines what they wished to say, but even that is dangerous, as then an actor can invest an importance that isn't intended. It is very difficult for me

to differentiate for a reader between lines that are important, and those lines that aren't. That's an element of the
craft of playwriting that I've never mastered. I don't know
how to show on the page unimportant lines versus more
significant lines.

DJ: What I have learned from this is that hopefully nearly
thirty per cent of the play feels so spontaneous and natural
and overlapped and half-sentenced that you do get an illusion
of almost totally naturalistic dialogue raised to an art form.
What I love about your scenes starting in the middle, is
that it corresponds with my film background because what
you do when you shoot a scene is you shoot the beginning,
the middle and the end and you go into the cutting room
and you cut the head and the tail off to get to the meat.
Film enables you to cut right into the middle of things.
For the actor to find out what note to hit with those first
lines, we had to do a variety of improvisations, particularly
before the lobby scene when they come in from the barri-
cades outside, and we did very simplistic things like running
around the rehearsal room three times and coming through
obstacles to arrive in the lobby.

RN: You understood that it was important for me not to be
there. There is logic to the beginning of the scenes and in the
discovery of that logic you have to make a lot of mistakes, you
have to be wrong before you can be right.
    Since we last worked on stage, I've been drawn into the
rehearsal process in a much more vocal and participatory
way. Jack O'Brien, who directed *Two Shakespearean Actors*
in New York, told me, 'Honey, if you don't jump in when
you see something wrong, I'm gonna see a void and I'm
gonna fill it.' John Caird on *Columbus* would say to me in
front of twenty-five actors, 'Richard, what do you think?
What did you mean?' I would try to explain and a process
was developed where after three or four weeks people could
completely disagree with me and go on their merry way and I

was happy with that. It was useful because I'm not the best interpreter of my work, I'm not a director and I can be wrong about what my work is about. There's some distance between the man who wrote the play and the man in rehearsal even if only in terms of time.

DJ: You put your finger on it when you say you are not necessarily the best interpreter of your play. On the other hand I don't think there's any doubt that you are the best understander of the play.

I have also changed since we last worked together. The example you give about no chair for you to sit on is apt. I am much less solicitous about you in rehearsal. I think you're a big boy and can look after yourself. Up to and including *Principia* I worried about you a lot in rehearsal. I thought you must be going crazy sitting there all the time and I must find ways to involve you. I don't think that any more because I know if you're bored you're going to go away.

I think the change in our relationship came when we were doing the television production of *Sensibility and Sense*, where inevitably I was not so much directing the actors as going for camera shots, and for you it was a very strange new process. You didn't know what the hell I was up to at certain times, or indeed how the scene was going to look. Nevertheless your presence was invaluable. Probably, you felt that I was less in touch with you in rehearsals than I had been before.

RN: Because of the circumstance of *Sensibility and Sense* – the fact that you were putting on a brand new play in three weeks, with only a week and a half rehearsal and another week and a half for your camera script – I never had the opening to give my notes and suddenly it was gone. Something of the same thing happened with the first production of *Two Shakespearean Actors*. It got away from me and I didn't know how. So I changed. I realized I had to be, and I wished to be, a bit more independent from the director. I realized I had stakes, I could talk with producers or with actors but in a reasonable way. So the rehearsal room became a different place for me in the way that's evolved with Jack O'Brien and with John Caird and, I think, with you. This is a very interesting growing up experience. We didn't know each other at the beginning of *Misha's Party* even though we knew each other better than anyone else in the theatre. Time had passed and we were feeling each other out. You were able to change; you were able to look, you were able to hear. The comment that I waited for in rehearsal, probably more than any other, you made once pretty early on and then you made it three or four times in the first two weeks and it was, 'We play this play fast.' You didn't hesitate to say that, because you heard the music right away and you played it, and the moment I heard that I didn't care how long anything was in rehearsal, I just knew you were hearing it and that's the bottom line for me and why in the last weeks of rehearsal there was nothing for me to do and I could go away.

I remember one actor saying how rare it was at the RSC to get notes in which you're not only told what you're doing wrong but where you're told what you're doing right. For a writer sitting in on notes to hear what's right is even more important. That's the communication that I have with you. We don't have to speak, we don't have to go to the pub.

DJ: Because I could stop worrying about you I rehearsed the inset scenes very close up and I rehearsed the group scenes in a much more televisual manner, moving around all the time, so it wasn't like the usual relationship of you and I sitting next to each other at one end of a rehearsal room. You spoke up much more and I think I asked you to speak more about what scenes were about and that is always terrific.

I think the only time when I'd say, 'Just back off,' is when I'm working with an actor who I know is having a lot of problems with a scene and all I'm trying to get is *one* of the five colours right. I can see you thinking, 'Does David really think that's what the scene's about?' but what I'm trying to do is build that layer and then come onto another layer. If we start to tell the actor right then that there are five layers they're going to get anxious.

The other point is that people don't understand, because it's not our job to show it in public, how insecure directors are for about half of the rehearsal. They really don't know if they've got the scene right, or if they know what the scene should be, they don't know how to get the actors to do the scene. There was only one instance, I think, towards the end of rehearsal when because it was a scene I knew I hadn't cracked yet, I snapped at you.

I need reaction time, and often I feel the comment means 'the whole production is a disaster' so I have to live with that, absorb it, give it proportion, think, 'How can I feed that in?' What I can't do is jump immediately from comment straight over to the actor and say, 'Now we do this.'

RN: No one would expect that. If I have a comment, it's very hard to know how it will be heard. If it's a small comment I don't know how to say, 'This is a small comment,' but –

DJ: As Freud said, 'There are no small comments.' I'm a little bit less temperamental than some people but I know I can be frosty. The great thing is you have persistence and stubbornness and you won't take it from me, you come back to me. I can imagine some wilting violets who wouldn't do that. I very rarely snap at actors. I will occasionally, if they come back a fifth time on a problem that's been solved weeks ago but on the whole, maybe I over-indulge? I don't think so, because what one gets out of that degree of support and encouragement is worth every bit of what you put in.

RN: With the playwright–director relationship it must be a relationship that avoids blame.

DJ: We are an old marriage and it means we can get mad with each other in public and we can make fun of each other in public and the company sensed within twenty minutes of seeing us together that we were a single unit. I don't think at any point in *Misha's Party* there was a sense of the author and director speaking with different voices at different times. Also, because we were so close, we didn't have to be respectful to each other and they weren't overawed either by you or by me. I think they knew we were a team that knew each other backwards and I think they believed that I understood what you wanted to write and you believed in my ability to make that happen. It made for a very positive rehearsal room atmosphere. Maybe one can build up a stronger formula – that at the end of each day we have a little talk – but you and I don't quite operate like that.

RN: I think a formula would be a mistake because it becomes a duty. I've had experiences where the director gives off the feeling, 'Oh, you want your time. I will now listen to your notes,' and you feel like you're nothing, like you're just being listened to for the sake of the director's self-righteousness.

DJ: We did have a specific new wrinkle to our relationship on *Misha's Party* in that it was a co-authorship project. And something has rubbed off onto your writing simply from the time spent with Gelman and spent in Russia. There is an openness, a vitality, an energy, an anarchy about some of this writing which I think is a new dimension for you. Although I know your style I had to relearn your style. The way you notated this play, and the dialogue, it's like a painter finding a new technique of putting stuff down on the page.

You have your normal battery of silences where what is underneath the surface comes through but what I think is new here is your double-dash notation and the number of unfinished sentences. What you have continually is something that appears inconclusive but is actually to do with, 'The words are redundant. I have got the sense through, why finish the sentence?' which is the way we talk. The marvellous thing about the little dashes – once you explained they were interruptions either by another character or more often of thought processes within the person talking – is that they're nearly always little censorships or little dissatisfactions with what has been said and improvements on them. I discovered the whole fizz of the play was to take those on.

It was very interesting when the actors were trying to crank up to speed in the last week of rehearsal – slightly artificially – that it was then that we almost lost the quality of those hesitations and I said, 'The play is like a stream. Those tiny pauses, of which there are maybe ten on a page, are like the little rocks that give the stream its strength.' We had a company who by their basic instinct realized they were dealing with an extraordinary style and they better learn it the right way because if they tried to redo it in any kind of way they were in trouble. I think they have been amazingly loyal, not just to the words, which is one thing, but much more importantly to the musical notation which you put down.

It's a delight to see a new form of theatre painting in the way you've written the dialogue. I think it's major and I think it's an innovation.

RN: Thank you. It's part of the evolution of our history. For a long time, in the last ten or fifteen years, I've tried to do those two things, to get more and more people into my plays and to under-write more and more. What I hoped to get out of *Misha's Party* was to continue my work with large casts – of fourteen or fifteen – so that what's unique about the music is you have so many people on stage. If you had two people on stage, that music is different; if you have four it's different again.

DJ: Absolutely.

RN: The essence of whether the playwright–director relationship continues is that both parties are willing to change.

[The Sunday reviews for *Misha's Party* were much better, and the magazines even better, with *Time Out* giving the play and production a highly favourable review. The play sold-out its run at The Pit.]

Biographical Note: David Jones

1934
Born Poole, Dorset. Father a Congregational minister. Mother a mathematician.

1951–4
Attended Christ's College Cambridge, where he acted in many of Peter Hall's undergraduate productions.

1954–6
National Service: 2nd Lieutenant RA. Served in Hong Kong, where he played title role in *Othello*, and was newsreader for Radio Hong Kong.

1958–64
Directed more than twenty half-hour documentary films for the BBC's first television arts magazine programme, *Monitor*, including profiles of the Berliner Ensemble, Theatre Workshop and of the writers William Golding, E. M. Forster and Lawrence Durrell. Responsible for studio direction of some fifty editions of *Monitor*, including regular presentation of ten-minute extracts from new London plays.
Editor of *Monitor* 1962–4.

1961
First London production, at the Mermaid Theatre; a triple bill of T. S. Eliot's *Sweeney Agonistes*, W. B. Yeats's *Purgatory* and Samuel Beckett's *Krapp's Last Tape*.

1962
Directed *The Empire Builders* by Boris Vian in the RSC's new play season at the Arts Theatre, London.

1964
Compiled and directed *Farewell to the Vic*, a 75-minute television documentary tribute to the Old Vic when it became the home of the National Theatre.
Invited by Peter Hall to join the RSC as Artistic Controller.

1965
The Governor's Lady by David Mercer (RSC, Aldwych Theatre, London)
The Investigation by Peter Weiss (RSC, co-directed with Peter Brook at the Aldwych Theatre, London)
Saint's Day by John Whiting (Stratford East Theatre, London)

Introduced on television the series *The Present Stage*, featuring the work of John Osborne, Harold Pinter, Arnold Wesker and Samuel Beckett.

1966
Belcher's Luck by David Mercer (RSC, Aldwych Theatre, London)
Becomes Associate Director of the RSC.

1967
As You Like It (RSC, Stratford-upon-Avon/Aldwych; in 1968 Los Angeles/Stratford-upon-Avon)

1968
The Tempest (Chichester Festival Theatre)
Diary of a Scoundrel by Alexander Ostrovsky (Liverpool Playhouse)
Wrote and directed for television *I Am*, a film biography of the poet John Clare.

1969
The Silver Tassie by Sean O'Casey (RSC, Aldwych)

RSC company director for London (1969–72).

1970
After Haggerty by David Mercer (RSC, Aldwych/Criterion Theatre, London)
The Plebeians Rehearse the Uprising by Günther Grass (RSC, Aldwych)

1971
Enemies by Maxim Gorky, translated by Jeremy Brooks and Kitty Hunter Blair (RSC, Aldwych)

1972
The Lower Depths by Maxim Gorky, translated by Jeremy Brooks and Kitty Hunter Blair (RSC, Aldwych)
The Island of the Mighty by John Arden and Margaretta D'Arcy (RSC, Aldwych)

1973
Directed for television *An Artist's Story* by Anton Chekhov, adapted
by Jeremy Brooks, and *Barbara of the House of Grebe* by Thomas
Hardy, adapted by David Mercer.
Love's Labour's Lost (RSC, Stratford-upon-Avon)

1974
Duck Song by David Mercer (RSC, Aldwych)
Summerfolk by Maxim Gorky, translated by Jeremy Brooks and
Kitty Hunter Blair (RSC, Aldwych)

1975
Summerfolk and *Love's Labour's Lost* (Brooklyn Academy of Music
(BAM) Theatre Company, New York)
Twelfth Night (Stratford Festival Theatre, Ontario)
The Marrying of Anne Leete by Harley Granville-Barker (RSC,
Aldwych)
The Return of A. J. Raffles by Graham Greene (RSC, Aldwych)

Wins an Obie Award for *Summerfolk*.
Appointed RSC Artistic Director of the Aldwych (1975–7).

1976
The Zykovs by Maxim Gorky, translated by Jeremy Brooks and
Kitty Hunter Blair (RSC, Aldwych)
Ivanov by Anton Chekhov, translated by Jeremy Brooks and Kitty
Hunter Blair (RSC, Aldwych)

1977
All's Well That Ends Well (Stratford Festival Theatre, Ontario)

Appointed Producer of BBC TV's *Play of the Month* (to 1978);
presented *You Never Can Tell* by George Bernard Shaw, *Waste*
by Harley Granville-Barker, *The Seagull* by Anton Chekhov,
Flint by David Mercer, *The Sea* by Edward Bond, *Kean* by Jean-
Paul Sartre, *Marya* by Isaac Babel, *The Voysey Inheritance*
by Harley Granville-Barker and *Danton's Death* by George
Büchner.

1978
Directed for television *The Beaux Stratagem* by George Farquhar
and *Ice Age* by Tankred Dorst.

Directed *Langrishe, Go Down*, a film script by Harold Pinter, adapted from the novel by Aidan Higgins.

1979
Cymbeline (RSC, Stratford-upon-Avon)
Baal by Bertolt Brecht (RSC, The Other Place, Stratford-upon-Avon/The Warehouse, London)

Becomes Artistic Director of the Brooklyn Academy of Music (BAM) Theatre Company.
Meets Richard Nelson and asks him to become BAM's Literary Manager.

1980
The Winter's Tale (BAM)
Barbarians by Maxim Gorky, translated by Jeremy Brooks and Kitty Hunter Blair (BAM)

Wins a second Obie, with Richard Nelson, for 'Innovative Programming' for BAM.

1981
A Midsummer Night's Dream (BAM)
Jungle of Cities by Bertolt Brecht, adapted by Richard Nelson (BAM)
Rip Van Winkle or The Works by Richard Nelson (Yale Repertory Theatre)

1983
The Custom of the Country by Nicholas Wright (RSC, The Pit, London)
Directs film of *Betrayal* by Harold Pinter, produced by Sam Spiegel.
Directs for the BBC TV's 'Shakespeare Series' (1983–4) *The Merry Wives of Windsor* and *Pericles*.

1984
Tramway Road by Ronald Harwood (Lyric Theatre, London)

1985
Old Times by Harold Pinter (Theatre Royal, London/St Louis and Henry Fonda Theatre, Los Angeles)

Wins LA Critics Dramalogue Award for Best Direction for *Old Times*.

1986
Principia Scriptoriae by Richard Nelson (RSC, The Pit, London)
The Devil's Disciple by George Bernard Shaw (TV)

1987
84 Charing Cross Road, film by Hugh Whitemore from the book by Helen Hanff, produced by Mel Brooks
Between East and West by Richard Nelson (Hampstead Theatre, London)

1988
The Christmas Wife, adapted by William Nicholson (HBO)

1989
Jacknife, a film by Steve Metcalfe
Look Back in Anger by John Osborne (Thames Television)

1990
Barbarians by Maxim Gorky (RSC, Barbican, London)
In My Defence by Jack Emery (BBC 2)

1991
A Fire in the Dark by David Hill (CBS)

1992
The Trial, a film adapted by Harold Pinter from the book by Franz Kafka, produced by Louis Marks and Kobi Jaeger

1993
Misha's Party by Richard Nelson and Alexander Gelman (RSC, The Pit, London)
No Man's Land by Harold Pinter (Roundabout Theatre, New York)

1994
And Then There Was One by Rama Laurie Stagner (Lifetime Channel)
Picket Fences (two episodes) by David Kelly (CBS)
Is There Life Out There? by Dalene Young (CBS)
Message for Posterity by Dennis Potter (BBC TV)

Biographical Note: Richard Nelson

1950
Born, Chicago, Illinois.

1968–72
Attended Hamilton College, Clinton, New York, where he wrote
and had produced fourteen plays (mostly one-acts).

1972–3
Awarded a Thomas J. Watson Travel Fellowship; lived in
Manchester, England, for a year.

1975
The Killing of Yablonski (Mark Taper Forum/Lab, Los Angeles),
first professional production.

1976
Conjuring an Event (Mark Taper Forum/Lab, Los Angeles)
Scooping (Arena Stage, Washington DC)

1977
Conjuring an Event (Williamstown Theatre Festival, Mass.)

1978
The Killing of Yablonski is given mainstage production at the PAF
Playhouse, Long Island.
Conjuring an Event (American Place Theatre, New York), first
production in New York City.
Jungle Coup (Playwrights Horizons, New York)

Receives Rockefeller Grant for Playwriting.
Receives National Endowment for the Arts Grant for Playwriting.

1979
The Vienna Notes (Guthrie Theatre II, Minneapolis/Playwrights
Horizons, New York)
Don Juan adaptation from Molière (Arena Stage, Washington)

The Vienna Notes wins an Obie Award for Playwriting.

Meets David Jones.
Appointed Literary Manager of the Brooklyn Academy of Music
(BAM) Theatre Company.

1980
Bal is given mainstage production at the Goodman Theatre, Chicago.
The Wedding adaptation from Brecht (BAM)
The Suicide adaptation from Erdmann (Goodman Theatre, Chicago)
Il Campiello adaptation from Goldoni (Acting Company)

Wins Obie Award, with David Jones, for 'Innovative Programming'
for the BAM Theatre Company.
Appointed Associate Director (part-time) of the Goodman Theatre,
Chicago.

1981
Jungle of Cities adaptation from Brecht (BAM) is directed by
David Jones.
Rip Van Winkle or The Works (Yale Repertory Theatre) is directed
by David Jones.

Appointed Dramaturge of the Guthrie Theatre, Minneapolis (Liviu
Ciulei, Artistic Director). Leaves after one year.

1982
The Marriage of Figaro adaptation from Beaumarchais (Guthrie
Theatre, Minneapolis)
The Return of Pinocchio (Bay Area Playwrights Festival,
California)
The Vienna Notes (Sheffield Crucible Theatre Studio),
first production in England

1983
An American Comedy is given mainstage production at the Mark
Taper Forum, Los Angeles.
The Return of Pinocchio (Empty Space Theatre, Seattle)

Awarded Guggenheim Grant.

1984
Between East and West (Seattle Rep/Studio)
Three Sisters adaptation from Chekhov (Guthrie Theatre,
Minneapolis)

Accidental Death of an Anarchist adaptation from Fo (Arena Stage, Washington/on Broadway)

1985
Between East and West (Yale Repertory Theatre)
The Marriage of Figaro (Circle in the Square, on Broadway)

1986
Principia Scriptoriae (Manhattan Theatre Club, New York; and, directed by David Jones, RSC, The Pit, London)

Wins HBO Award for *Between East and West*.
Wins ABC Award for *Principia Scriptoriae*.
Awarded a two-year NEA Play-writing Fellowship.

1987
Principia is produced in Bremen, Germany, Nelson's first European production.
Languages Spoken Here is presented on BBC Radio 4, Nelson's first radio play.
Some Americans Abroad is commissioned by the RSC, Nelson's first commission.
Between East and West (Hampstead Theatre, London) is directed by David Jones.

Wins a London *Time Out* Award for *Principia*.

1988
Chess (author of the book of the musical) is produced on Broadway.
Roots in Water (River Arts Repertory Theatre, New York)

Wins Giles Cooper Award for *Languages Spoken Here*.
Awarded second Rockefeller Grant for Playwriting.

1989
Some Americans Abroad (RSC, The Pit, London)
Eating Words presented on BBC Radio 3
Jitterbugging adaptation of *La Ronde* (River Arts Rep, New York)

Wins Giles Cooper Award for *Eating Words*.
Some Americans Abroad is joint-winner of *Plays and Players* Play of the Year Award.

1990
Some Americans Abroad (Lincoln Center Theatre)
Works on *King, The Musical*, then quits.
Sensibility and Sense presented nationally on PBS television,
produced by American Playhouse, directed by David Jones.
Advice to Eastern Europe presented on BBC Radio 4 and The
World Service.
Two Shakespearean Actors (RSC, Swan Theatre, Stratford-upon-
Avon)

Some Americans Abroad is nominated for an Olivier Award for Best
Comedy.

1991
The End of a Sentence is presented on PBS television by American
Playhouse, directed by David Jones.
Awarded the prestigious three-year Lila Wallace Reader's Digest
Writers Award.

1992
Two Shakespearean Actors (on Broadway, by Lincoln Center
Theatre)
Ethan Frome (screenplay) opens in the US, produced by American
Playhouse.
Columbus and the Discovery of Japan (RSC, Barbican, London)

Two Shakespearean Actors nominated for five TONY Awards,
including Best Play.

1993
Misha's Party, co-written with Russian playwright Alexander Gelman
and co-commissioned by the RSC and the Moscow Art Theatre, is
presented by the RSC at The Pit, London, directed by David Jones.
Life Sentences (Second Stage Theatre, New York)

1994
Misha's Party (Moscow Art Theatre, Russia)
New England (RSC, The Pit, London)
The American Wife is presented by the BBC on Radio 4.